Hamid Karzai

Hamid Karzai

by Viqi Wagner

LUCENT BOOKS
A part of Gale, Cengage Learning

GALE
CENGAGE Learning™

Detroit • New York • San Francisco • New Haven, Conn • Waterville, Maine • London

FEB 2 3 2012

© 2011 Gale, Cengage Learning

LIBRARY OF CONGRESS CATALOGING-IN-PUBLICATION DATA

Wagner, Viqi, 1953-
  Hamid Karzai / by Viqi Wagner.
    p. cm. -- (People in the news)
  Includes bibliographical references and index.
  ISBN 978-1-4205-0425-5 (hardcover)
  1. Karzai, Hamid, 1957---Juvenile literature. 2. Presidents--Afghanistan--Biography--Juvenile literature. 3. Afghanistan--Politics and government--2001---Juvenile literature. I. Title.
  DS371.43.K37W34 2011
  958.104'7092--dc22
  [B]
                                                                        2010043802

Lucent Books
27500 Drake Rd
Farmington Hills MI 48331

ISBN-13: 978-1-4205-0425-5
ISBN-10: 1-4205-0425-8

Printed in the United States of America
1 2 3 4 5 6 7 15 14 13 12 11

Printed by Bang Printing, Brainerd, MN, 1st Ptg., 03/2011

Contents

Fame and celebrity are alluring. People are drawn to those who walk in fame's spotlight, whether they are known for great accomplishments or for notorious deeds. The lives of the famous pique public interest and attract attention, perhaps because their experiences seem in some ways so different from, yet in other ways so similar to, our own.

Newspapers, magazines, and television regularly capitalize on this fascination with celebrity by running profiles of famous people. For example, television programs such as Entertainment Tonight devote all their programming to stories about entertainment and entertainers. Magazines such as People fill their pages with stories of the private lives of famous people. Even newspapers, newsmagazines, and television news frequently delve into the lives of well-known personalities. Despite the number of articles and programs, few provide more than a superficial glimpse at their subjects.

Lucent's People in the News series offers young readers a deeper look into the lives of today's newsmakers, the influences that have shaped them, and the impact they have had in their fields of endeavor and on other people's lives. The subjects of the series hail from many disciplines and walks of life. They include authors, musicians, athletes, political leaders, entertainers, entrepreneurs, and others who have made a mark on modern life and who, in many cases, will continue to do so for years to come.

These biographies are more than factual chronicles. Each book emphasizes the contributions, accomplishments, or deeds that have brought fame or notoriety to the individual and shows how that person has influenced modern life. Authors portray their subjects in a realistic, unsentimental light. For example, Bill Gates – the cofounder and chief executive officer of the software giant Microsoft – has been instrumental in making personal computers the most vital tool of the modern age. Few dispute his business savvy, his perseverance, or his technical expertise, yet critics say he is ruthless in his dealings with competitors and driven more by his desire to maintain Microsoft's dominance in the computer industry than by an interest in furthering technology.

In these books, young readers will encounter inspiring stories about real people who achieved success despite enormous obstacles. Oprah Winfrey – the most powerful, most watched, and wealthiest woman on television today – spent the first six years of her life in the care of her grandparents while her unwed mother sought work and a better life elsewhere. Her adolescence was colored by promiscuity, pregnancy at age fourteen, rape, and sexual abuse.

Each author documents and supports his or her work with an array of primary and secondary source quotations taken from diaries, letters, speeches, and interviews. All quotes are footnoted to show readers exactly how and where biographers derive their information and provide guidance for further research. The quotations enliven the text by giving readers eyewitness views of the life and accomplishments of each person covered in the People in the News series.

In addition, each book in the series includes photographs, annotated bibliographies, timelines, and comprehensive indexes. For both the casual reader and the student researcher, the People in the News series offers insight into the lives of today's newsmakers – people who shape the way we live, work, and play in the modern age.

The Afghan Partner in America's Longest War

In June 2010, U.S. news networks carried the dismal report that America's war in Afghanistan had surpassed the conflict in Vietnam to become the longest war in U.S. history. The news was not only sad but ironic because the international military coalition that went to war in Afghanistan on October 7, 2001, expected the battle to be decisive and short.

Hamid Karzai, president of Afghanistan, has been America's Afghan partner since the first days of the war. For Karzai, however, the war in Afghanistan began long before 2001. His country has been in a perpetual state of war for more than thirty years. Karzai has spent his entire adult life working to restore peace and unity to his war-torn country. As America's partner and as an Afghan patriot, he too wanted the U.S. war in Afghanistan to be decisive and short.

The Mission in Afghanistan

The current war's original mission was to find and destroy the leaders of the September 11, 2001, attacks, Osama bin Laden and his terrorist organization, al Qaeda, who were hiding in Afghanistan. The mission also aimed to destroy Afghanistan's harsh rulers, the Taliban. The Taliban and al Qaeda are Islamic extremists. They view democracies, such as the United States, as infidels—unbelievers who do not accept the one true god of Islam—and therefore enemies. The anti-American Taliban regime was protecting Bin Laden, al Qaeda, and many other militant Islamist groups and allowing them to operate terrorist training camps in Afghanistan.

Stunned and outraged by the September 11 attacks, world governments responded quickly to U.S. president George W. Bush's call for war in Afghanistan. On October 7, Bush announced the first air strikes on the Taliban by a U.S. and British-led

Hamid Karzai, once an exiled resistance fighter, was named interm chair fo the Afghan Transitional Authority (ATA) in December 2001.

coalition of more than forty-five countries. "We are supported," he told the American people, "by the collective will of the world."[1] Americans were also supported by an anti-Taliban uprising within Afghanistan, led in the south by Karzai. In exile in neighboring Pakistan when the war began, Karzai sneaked across the border and rallied his fellow Afghans to fight.

By mid-November 2001, coalition forces had driven the Taliban out of Kabul, the Afghan capital. In December, only eight weeks after the campaign began, Taliban leaders signed an unconditional surrender. Suddenly, Karzai the resistance fighter became Karzai the national leader. With the backing and goodwill of the international coalition and prominent Afghans inside and outside the country, Karzai was named president of a new, transitional government.

The popular Karzai went to work to prepare for Afghanistan's rebirth as a democratic state. Though Bin Laden was still at large, in October 2002 U.S. secretary of defense Donald Rumsfeld claimed the mission had been accomplished: "The Taliban are gone. The Al Qaeda are gone."[2] Coalition troops were deployed in Afghanistan to secure the country until a new Afghan army and police force could take over. The international community pledged billions of dollars in foreign aid. It seemed Karzai's life-long goal of Afghan peace and unity might finally be achieved.

Obstacles to Progress

Despite these positive steps, Afghans' optimism soon faded. One problem was that the war in Afghanistan was quickly overshadowed by the U.S. war in Iraq, which began in March 2003. The fighting in Iraq was intense and, at the time, a higher priority for the U.S. government. As a result, military and financial resources were diverted away from Afghanistan to Iraq. The coalition strength was reduced to a small, multinational peacekeeping force in Kabul. The Afghan conflict became known as "the other war." Its ongoing mission was unclear.

To militant extremists such as Bin Laden and the Taliban, however, the war in Afghanistan was far from over. In fact, Bin Laden had released a videotape on the first day of the war calling on all Muslims to rise up and destroy America and drive non-Muslims out of Afghanistan. "The wind of faith is blowing," he declared, and "America will not live in peace … before all the army of infidels depart the land of Islam."[3] The Islamist militants declared war not only on non-Muslims but also on Muslim governments that do not hold their extreme views or that have American or Western ties. Their obvious target in Afghanistan was the new, pro-American government led by Karzai, a moderate Muslim. Karzai kept warning his U.S. supporters that terrorism was still a real threat in his country, but the United States was focused on fighting terrorism elsewhere. The Taliban and other rebel groups took advantage of this situation. In 2004 they began a violent comeback in Kandahar Province in southern Afghanistan.

The Afghan people had faith in Karzai, though. They elected him to a five-year term as president in 2004. When weak Afghan government forces could not stop the spreading insurgency or protect Afghan civilians, however, public opinion turned against him. His reelection in 2009 was marred by corruption charges. His plans to rebuild Afghanistan stalled amid growing anti-American and anti-Karzai violence.

Thus, instead of a short, decisive war, both America and Karzai got something entirely different. As ABC News managing editor Thomas Nagorski writes,

> Here we are, nearly a decade since that October Sunday [in 2001], and the end of [the war] is hard to see, or fathom. Under the order of a new commander-in-chief, the U.S. is now 'surging' forces into Afghanistan; a new and complex mission looms in Kandahar; and the Taliban are 'surging' too, to devastating effect.[4]

The Right Man for the Job?

As the leader of the Afghan government forces, Karzai has been juggling the demands of all the combatants in the war for more than nine years. As president of Afghanistan—an ancient, multiethnic society with more than thirty languages—he governs 29 million people with their own needs and demands. He must do all this in a country that has been destroyed by decades of war. It may be an impossible task, but he has been trained since childhood to lead, and lead is what he intends to do.

Afghan political expert Haseeb Humayoon writes that "personalities rather than enduring and credible national institutions dictate the course of politics"[5] in Afghanistan. If that is so, perhaps strong-willed Karzai will be able to broker a truce long enough to rebuild his broken country and secure enough for America's longest war to end.

On the one hand, Karzai is the right man for this job. He is a true Afghan patriot who is passionately committed to democratic ideals and a peaceful resolution of the war. He has a deep understanding of the complicated ethnic and religious rifts in Afghan society. He also has an unshakeable belief in his ability to bring Afghans together again, despite their differences, for the good of Afghanistan.

On the other hand, Karzai is a mass of contradictions. He is secretive and open, idealistic and pragmatic, at times indecisive, and not always reliable. He loses his temper and makes rash threats when anyone questions his honesty or competence. He tolerates widespread corruption in his government. Moreover, to stop the violence, Karzai has offered to strike deals with the Taliban and other insurgents. American officials view this as cooperating with the enemy that is shooting at and killing U.S. soldiers. Other critics suggest Karzai is making shrewd deals with warlords and insurgents to keep himself in power, not to unify Afghanistan.

These contradictions partly explain why the relationship between Karzai and U.S. leaders has been increasingly stormy in recent years. If the United States does not have a trustworthy Afghan partner, there is little chance that American counterinsurgency or state-building efforts will succeed in Afghanistan. For now, however, U.S. officials seem willing to back Karzai because, according to Secretary of State Hillary Clinton, fighting terrorism in his country serves U.S. interests. Experts say there is another important reason why America backs Karzai: America has no other choice. As Pakistani political analyst Ishtiaq Ahmad points out, "There is … no other alternative Afghan leader whose past has been as non-controversial as Karzai's, or who is charismatic enough to win as much international goodwill as Karzai has."[6]

It remains to be seen how and when the war in Afghanistan will end. For better or worse, Hamid Karzai is likely to be the person who dictates the course. Karzai himself makes few predictions, except to say that his duty will not change: "Through it all my guiding principle has remained the same: work for Afghanistan. Very simple."[7]

Chapter 1

The Dutiful Son

Hamid Karzai was born into a family of leaders. The leadership model he was raised to follow, however, was the local khan, or tribal chief, not a democratically elected president or central government. The values he absorbed in childhood were those of conservative, traditional Sunni Muslims in Afghanistan's educated upper class.

Family Origins

Hamid Karzai was born on December 24, 1957, to tribal leader Abdul Ahad Karzai and his wife, Sarajo Karzai. The name *Karzai* means "from the village of Karz," where Hamid was born. Karz lies just outside the city of Kandahar, the capital of Afghanistan's southeastern Kandahar Province. The long eastern edge of this agricultural state is the poorly marked border between Afghanistan and Pakistan. For centuries, the gardens and orchards of Kandahar were famous for almonds, melons, and pomegranates.

The Karzais are members of the powerful Pashtuns, the largest ethnic group in Afghanistan. Hamid's father, like his father before him, was the khan, or chief, of the Popolzai clan of the Durrani Pashtun tribe. The title of khan is not just ceremonial. In Afghanistan, local khans have most of the political power and are the largest landowners. One or more khans settle disputes, arrange marriages, collect fees and taxes, and make decisions for the community according to traditional rules, without paperwork or signatures. Their authority comes from family status and strength of personality (backed up with weapons if necessary),

The orchards of Kandahar are famous for their pomegranates, which Karzai has called "the best in the world."

and their word is law.

One result of this way of governing is that public records are rare in Afghanistan. Most Afghans do not apply for marriage certificates from the government. Most births still occur at home, and no official birth certificate is issued or filed. What records there are consist of tribal record books kept by tribal elders or mullahs (religious teachers/leaders) according to sharia, or Islamic law. The availability and accuracy of this information varies widely. Many Afghans, for example, are not sure of the year they were born. Because the Karzai family is prominent and educated, however, much more has been recorded about them.

At the time of Hamid's birth, Afghanistan was a stable monarchy. The popular shah, or king, was Muhammad Zahir Shah, a Durrani Pashtun like the Karzais. Zahir Shah's royal line had ruled the country since the 1700s. Zahir Shah had ruled from the Arg Palace in Kabul since 1933. During his forty-year reign, he set out to make his country more democratic. His reforms included the creation of a new constitution and parliament, free elections, voting rights for women, and the country's first modern university. Despite some political quarrels among Afghanistan's major ethnic groups—Pashtuns in the south, Uzbeks and Tajiks in the north—Zahir Shah kept the peace.

Mohammad Zahir Shah, the last king of Afghanistan, was strongly supported by the Karzai family.

The Karzai family was a close supporter of Zahir Shah. They were members of the same tribe and related by marriage. Several of Hamid's relatives held important posts in the king's government. Hamid's grandfather, for example, served as deputy speaker of the Senate in the king's parliament. An uncle traveled with the king on a state visit to the United States to meet with President John F. Kennedy. He also served as Zahir Shah's advisor, speechwriter, and permanent representative to the United Nations (UN).

A Privileged but Strict Upbringing

Hamid was the middle son of eight children, seven sons and one daughter. From eldest to youngest, the Karzai siblings are Abdul Ahmed (born in 1949), followed by Qayum (1950), daughter Fouzia (1952), Mahmoud (1954), Hamid (1957), half brother Shah Wali (1959), half brother Ahmed Wali (1961), and Abdul Wali (1964).

Like 80 percent of the Afghan population, the Karzais are Sunni Muslim. Hamid's mother was an especially devout woman who fasted often. Karzai holds her up as a model of self-discipline and good values: "I learned a great deal about high moral standards from her."[8]

The Pashtuns in Afghan Society

Afghanistan, the ancient, landlocked country known as the crossroads of Asia, is a society of many ethnic groups and many languages. Some thirty languages are spoken in Afghanistan in addition to the two official languages, Pashto and Dari. Among the country's ethnic groups are Pashtun, Tajik, Uzbek, Hazara, Turkmen, Baluch, and Nuristani, each with its own complex ranks of kinship-based tribes and clans.

The Karzai family, like roughly 40 percent of Afghanistan's population, is Pashtun. The Pashtuns are concentrated in a wide swath over southern and eastern Afghanistan, overlapping into western Pakistan. They speak a common language, Pashto, and their ethnic identity is passed down through the father of the family; traditionally, only someone with a Pashtun father is Pashtun.

The Pashtuns have a celebrated history of kings and warriors. They also have a strong oral tradition; Pashtuns are renowned for their poets and storytellers. The greatest Pashtun heroes combined both skills: Seventeenth-century warrior-poet Kushal Khan Khattack, for example, united Pashtun armies to fight invaders from India and wrote more than two hundred books of poetry. Today, Afghan Pashtuns continue this tradition by expressing their approval or disapproval of President Karzai in verse.

The Karzai family is Pashtun. Pashtuns are spread over southern and eastern Afghanistan, and may be nomads, like these pictured.

The adult Karzai downplays his family's status in Kandahar Province: "We were not rich; there were many families in Kandahar who were far wealthier."[9] His biographer, Nick B. Mills, however, describes a standard of living far above that of most people in the Afghan countryside. Despite their privileges, the Karzai children were expected to follow their parents' strict rules: "The Karzais lived in a substantial house with a large garden. The family compound was large enough that Hamid could ride his horse inside the walls. The garden had fishponds, trees, and flowers. … His memories are of a comfortable life but a very disciplined one. The standards of behavior were quite rigid."[10]

Karzai recalls, however, that it was "an upbringing that has served me well in my life. … We learned to respect and obey not only our parents, but elders in general."[11]

The Karzai Home

Like upper-class families' homes all over Afghanistan, Hamid Karzai's home was a walled compound. The view from outside was just a high, blank, mud-brick wall; there was no beauty on display. Inside the wall, however, were courtyards and gardens and a main house with many rooms. Twig birdcages hung in the halls, filled with songbirds such as canaries and finches bought from bird sellers in the bazaar, or market. The adult Karzai romanticizes details like this, stressing Kandahar's natural beauty and abundance. British journalist Christina Lamb, an old friend of Karzai's, says she once visited Kandahar with Karzai "because of his rhapsodizing about its 40 varieties of grapes and pomegranates so sweet that poets wrote elegies to them."

Christina Lamb, "President of Hell: Hamid Karzai's Battle to Govern Post-war, Post-Taliban Afghanistan," *Sunday Times* (London), June 29, 2003. www.timesonline.co.uk/tol/life_and_style/article1143612.ece.

Early Education

Hamid grew up speaking Afghanistan's two official languages: Pashto, the Pashtun native tongue, and Dari (also known as Farsi or Afghan Persian). Dari is the first language of about half the Afghan population and the language of most formal communication in provincial and national government.

He says speaking both languages at home was an important example of the Afghan unity he wants to restore. To him it shows that Afghans once had a national identity, greater than their ethnic or tribal identity, that included speaking many different languages as a normal way of life:"Both languages were spoken and both languages were equally Afghan—there was no distinction. ... Nobody thought of Pashto as the language of only the Pashtuns and Farsi as the language of some other groups. No. They were the languages of Afghanistan. That's a very important point. We are bilingual but unicultural."[12]

Hamid began his schooling at the Mahmood Hotaki Elementary School in Kandahar. Then in 1965, when he was seven, his father was elected to represent Kandahar in the king's parliament. The Karzai family moved to Kabul when Hamid finished second grade.

From Kandahar to Kabul

Six thousand feet (1.8km) above sea level in east-central Afghanistan, Kabul sits in a high valley in the beautiful mountain ranges of the Hindu Kush. The sun shines three hundred days a year in this semiarid region, known for hot, dry summers and very cold winters.

In the 1960s, the capital was a clean, safe, cosmopolitan city of modern buildings and tree-lined boulevards. It boasted an excellent public transportation system and plenty of good restaurants. It was a favorite post for Western diplomats, who enjoyed the spectacular scenery, blue skies, and exotic customs of tribal Afghans. In the 1960s, Kabul also attracted adventurers and wanderers in search of Afghanistan's famous opium, but the rise of drug lords and Afghan heroin trafficking was still years away.

Kabul sits in the shadows of the Hindu Kush mountain range.

Hamid led a privileged but sheltered life in Kabul. He had a small circle of friends approved by his parents, who kept close track of the boys' activities. There was no lack of entertainment, however. Hamid and his friends went to the movies, rode bicycles around town, listened to Western pop music, and played soccer, cricket, and baseball. Once a year, the family vacationed in Istalif, an oasis about an hour outside the city. Hamid loved those visits: "All the kids in the extended family would be there, all of my cousins ... and we would stay for three or four days, running around, climbing trees, playing in the streams. ... Those outings were the most fun times of my childhood."[13]

The adult Karzai admits he was lucky: "By Afghan standards, we were a very well off family. The kind of life we had ... was really too good for the countries around us—big homes and lots of fun.…We had as much access to good music and movies—which at that age people really want—as any kid would have in Europe or America, and a good education."[14]

Two Kinds of Education

Hamid continued his studies in Kabul at the Sayed Jamaluddin Afghan School and the British-Afghan Habibia High School, both favorites of upper-class Afghan families. Quiet and studious, he thought about following in his father's footsteps in the parliament one day but says his teenage interests were not political: "I was very science oriented. I was doing very good in chemistry, and I went towards books about the evolution of mankind. Studies of Darwin." Hamid also became an avid reader. In addition to Iranian magazines and Afghan history books, he read translations of Western literature: "I was interested in Russian writers, like Anton Chekhov and Dostoyevsky, and also the English writers [such as] Charles Dickens."[15]

Hamid got another kind of education outside of school. In addition to his duties as an elected official, his father, Abdul Ahad Karzai, was still khan of the Popolzai clan, a clan of a half-million people, and was still called on to settle tribal disputes. Local matters were usually handled in a special guest room at the Karzai home in Kabul. Complicated disputes between members of different clans, however, required the senior Karzai to travel to distant villages for a council of male tribal elders, called a jirga. Sometimes he took Hamid with him.

The traditional way one such quarrel was solved had a powerful influence on Hamid's own presidential style. At the jirga, the tribal elders listened respectfully as both sides in the quarrel presented their arguments. Then Karzai's father and the other chiefs met privately to discuss the case. As Karzai recalls, "When they had arrived at a decision … they called the two sides together and told them, 'This is how it will be.' Both sides accepted the decision, and that settlement stands to this very day."[16]

The End of the Monarchy

A lot changed for Hamid's father in 1973. On July 16, while Zahir Shah was away in Italy, his cousin Prince Muhammad Daoud seized power in a nonviolent coup. The king went into exile in Rome. Daoud did not name himself the new king, however. Ending centuries of tradition, he abolished the monarchy and declared Afghanistan a republic, with himself as president. Hamid's father remained in the government, but from then on, his future was uncertain because of his close ties to the deposed king.

Daoud had his own plan for government and economic reform. He enlarged and modernized the army, which had supported him in the coup. He replaced the parliament with a council of appointed, not elected, officials. He also tried to steer Afghanistan away from Islamic extremism, a movement that was growing all over the Middle East.

Daoud had a complicated relationship with the Soviet Union (the USSR, or Russia), Afghanistan's superpower neighbor to the north. The Soviet Union's political system was communism. This system was based on an antireligious, powerful central government; rule by a dictator; and state ownership of land. Communism was completely at odds with Afghan traditions of fiercely independent tribes and devotion to Islam.

The Soviet Union's goal was to spread communism to other countries by revolution. It did this by supporting communist movements around the globe. One such movement was the Afghan Communist Party, known as the PDP. Daoud had the Afghan Communists' support in the coup. As president, he also negotiated deals for advanced weapons with the Soviet Union. The former prince was not a communist himself, however. Over time he distanced himself from Russia. He became a strong opponent of the PDP and fired PDP officials from important posts in his government.

From Afghanistan to India

Whatever political infighting went on in the Daoud government

Pashtunwali: The Afghan Code of Honor, Hospitality, and Revenge

As a Pashtun, Karzai is expected to abide by an unwritten, centuries-old social code called Pashtunwali. Part way of life and part code of justice, Pashtunwali governs both tribal affairs and individual conduct.

The nine basic duties of Pashtunwali are hospitality, asylum (providing safety and protection), justice/revenge, bravery, loyalty, righteousness (which Karzai often refers to as "a higher moral standard"), trust in Allah, honor and dignity for oneself, and honor of women. *Washington Post* associate editor David Ignatius explains the rituals of settling conflicts under Pashtunwali:

> Conflicts start because of an insult to a tribe's honor, which requires a rite of revenge known as *badal*. The fighting continues until scores are settled and the combatants are exhausted. ... Reconciliation begins with a process of repentance, known as *nanawatey*, in which the penitent party goes into the house of his rival and asks for asylum. In Pashtun culture, such a request must be granted; to spurn it would be shameful. Once the desire for an honorable peace is clear, the tribal elders gather in jirga [council meeting] and frame a temporary truce, known as a *teega*. The parties gather, agree to pay reparations, and the Pashtun code of generous hospitality, known as *melmastia*, takes over.

David Ignatius, "Afghan Reconciliation Strategy Should Reflect Pashtun Culture," *Washington Post*, May 16, 2010. www.washingtonpost.com/wp-dyn/content/article/2010/05/14/AR2010051404320.html.

had little effect on the day-to-day life of the Karzai family. Hamid continued his studies and obeyed his elders. Like most young people, he sometimes felt tied down by the restrictions and duties placed on him as the son of a Pashtun khan. He dreamed of escaping the tradition-bound rituals of tribal life and serving his country instead as a diplomat in the West.

In 1976 Hamid got his chance to see the world beyond Afghanistan. He graduated from Habibia High School and set his sights on attending college in India. One of his cousins was in Delhi studying medicine, so Hamid met him there, expecting to enroll in classes himself. He soon found, however, that he could not stand the climate. He was used to high and dry Kabul, not the monsoons and 114°F (45°C) heat waves of subtropical Delhi. His cousin suggested he apply instead to the university in Shimla, India, a city in the foothills of the Himalayas, 520 miles (837km) east of Kabul.

To Hamid, the train ride from Delhi to Shimla was like climbing to paradise. Shimla lies more than 7,200 feet (2,205m) above sea level amid lush forests. Summers are pleasant, winters cold and snowy. Hamid felt right at home. He applied and was accepted to Shimla's Himachal Pradesh University.

As much as he liked Shimla, his early months at the university were lonely. He was the only Afghan student there, and up to this point, he had had very limited direct contact with anyone outside his family. He was socially awkward and very reserved, always careful not to say anything that might offend anyone. Eventually, however, Hamid relaxed, made friends, and joined both social activities and discussion groups. Like college students everywhere in the 1970s, he grew long hair and wore bell-bottom jeans.

His typical daily routine began with an hour-long walk from his boardinghouse to the campus. After the day's classes and the long walk back, he ate a simple supper at a local hut before hitting the books in his room. He saw his family only on short trips back to Kabul at the end of a school term. He had fewer comforts than he enjoyed at home. Nevertheless, he remembers his time at the university as six exhilarating, wonderful years.

New Accomplishments and New Tastes

One of Hamid's major accomplishments at Himachal Pradesh was

The city of Shimla, India, lies in the foothills of the Himalayas. Karzai felt right at home in the snowy winters.

becoming fluent in four more languages: English, Urdu, Hindi, and French. Most of his classes were taught in English, so he had to scramble to pick up the vocabulary. He also had to work hard to catch up to the Indian students in laboratory work. Karzai recalls, however, that his education in Kabul had put him and his fellow students in Kabul "miles ahead" of his Indian classmates in general knowledge: "We were tops in mathematics, in physics, in chemistry—all the formulas, the elements, we knew those by heart. ... We had also studied American history, the Napoleonic Wars, current affairs, and I knew far more about these things, and about the Amazon and the Mississippi, for example, than my Indian counterparts."[17]

During the colonial era, when the British ruled India, Shimla was India's summer capital. British administrators and military officials and their families went to the beautiful, high-altitude retreat to escape from the sweltering heat of India's cities. The outpost was famous for its European-style buildings, side by side with ornate Hindu temples, and its British atmosphere was still strong in Hamid's day.

In Shimla, Hamid adopted some of the refined habits and lifestyle of the British. For example, he rented a room in one of the guesthouse mansions that the British once used as a summer cottage. He acquired courtly manners and British-accented English like that of an English gentleman. He developed a taste for Cadbury chocolates, British movies and television shows, English leather shoes, and the English novelist Somerset Maugham and poet Alfred Lord Tennyson.

Role Models

Hamid was also developing the values that would shape his political views and figuring out what kind of person he wanted to be. In his reading and study of international politics at Himachal Pradesh, he was most impressed by political leaders who had achieved great social change or triumphed over injustice through nonviolence. Among his favorites were South African leader Nelson Mandela and American civil rights leader Martin Luther King, Jr. The statesman who became his lifelong role model was Mohandas (Mahatma) Gandhi, the Indian independence leader who became a global symbol of nonviolent resistance:

> When I became an adult and began to know the world more, Gandhi was somebody that I admired very much. … I'm most affected by Gandhi. The struggle for independence of his country and the way he did it through peaceful means: non-violence, and the tolerance that he preached. And the way he respected mankind as a whole, and his self-restraint. A wonderful human being.[18]

Karzai also includes his father as an important role model and names the qualities in his father he admired most:

> His parliamentary elections, his conduct with the tribes. We are a tribal people, and the way his house would be open to people all the time was something that came automatically. And his love for peace. He hated violence. That was something that I admired in him a lot. He hated guns very much.[19]

Mohandas K. "Mahatma" Gandhi led a successful campaign of nonviolent resistance against British rule in India.

Karzai's Personality

Hamid's personality was taking shape as well. Some of his character traits were those he most admired in others and aspired to live up to—he was a tolerant, peace-loving young man. Hamid's basic nature was also dreamy and theatrical. According to journalist Elizabeth Rubin, "'The mad one,' that's how his father called him. The pet name stuck. A quiet boy, a dreamer, an odd one who could scare the other boys with his strange faces and moods, who loved to jump on his horse in jeans and cowboy boots and ride around as if in an American movie."[20]

His brother and sister describe Hamid as an idealistic and principled person. "By nature, Hamid is a very optimistic person, a person who thinks almost anything can be worked out,"[21] says Qayum Karzai. Sister Fouzia Royan says simply, "Hamid is a democrat."[22]

Qayum also says there is a strongly emotional, sentimental side to Hamid's personality: "He always had an enormously soft heart. ... Beggars used to come to our house and ask for Hamid."[23] The Karzai family seems to view Hamid as the sensitive middle brother who has big dreams and cries in public, and the siblings rally around him protectively now as they have since he was a boy.

In 1978 Hamid Karzai turned twenty-one. That year marked both the end of his youth and the end of peace in Afghanistan. It was the beginning of a perpetual state of war in his country and the beginning of what Karzai calls his life's struggle.

Chapter 2

Driving Out a Superpower

Beginning in 1978, Afghanistan was plunged into one disastrous war after another. As the violence and destruction worsened, Hamid Karzai's political activism and leadership skills took nonviolent forms. He brokered meetings between rival factions, raised funds and international awareness, worked for reconciliation, and sometimes just stayed out of the fight.

The Saur Revolution

In April 1978 (the month of Saur in the Afghan calendar), while Karzai was home in Kabul on a school break, the Afghan Communists launched a revolution and overthrew the Daoud government. President Daoud, who had made enemies by trying to get rid of PDP members in his government, was assassinated.

The new communist regime was shaky from the start. The communists tried to enact wildly unpopular reforms, including suppressing religious practices and seizing tribal lands. Violent protests broke out all over Afghanistan in the name of defending Islam against the communists. More political intrigue and coups followed; three more presidents were assassinated between April 1978 and December 1979.

Karzai had returned to college in India when the revolution started. The turmoil in Afghanistan made communication with his family difficult and telephone calls impossible. Hamid stayed

Crowd of Afghans storm prison shouting anti-Soviet slogans after the Marxist government released fewer political prisoners than expected in Pul-I-Charkhi.

put, opting to enroll in the master's degree program in political science after he finished his undergraduate studies. He was out of harm's way when the communist regime began violent purges of Afghan intellectuals, tribal chiefs, clerics, and anyone else with ties to the old monarchy. Karzai's father and uncle were not so fortunate. Karzai was shocked to learn that they had been arrested and thrown into the Pul-i-Charkhi prison, a place infamous for torturing and killing political prisoners during the communists' rule.

The Soviet Invasion of Afghanistan

On Christmas Day 1979, Karzai got another shock:

One morning when I was going to my university ... the newspapers said that the Soviet Union has invaded Afghanistan. My feeling at that moment suddenly was of a loss. I felt smaller. Much, much smaller than I felt before. ... I heard people talk about this invasion and suddenly I felt a loss of identity. Who am I? Do I have a country? Do I have a name? Do I have an identity? I said, "No, I don't. I don't have a country. My country is taken over."[24]

Within two weeks, there were one hundred thousand Soviet troops and eighteen hundred tanks in Afghanistan. Soviet leaders claimed their forces were only there at the request of the struggling Afghan Communist government. Then the Soviets murdered the Afghan president and set out to crush the anti-communist uprising. The operation was supposed to be quick. Instead, the Soviet invasion only made the rebellion worse.

On one side of the conflict was the Afghan Communist army, backed by the military might of the giant Soviet Union. On the other side were Afghan rebel groups called the mujahideen, who viewed the communist Soviets as aggressors and religious infidels. Also involved was the United States, the world's other military superpower. The United States and the Soviet Union were enemies, and the United States was committed to stopping the spread of communism around the globe. To this end, the U.S. government backed the mujahideen with weapons, money, and training in guerrilla warfare.

The mujahideen had other supporters, too: extremist Islamist militants from other countries who wanted to help the Afghan Muslims resist the Soviet occupation. These Islamist militants believed in using jihad, or holy war, to drive out Westerners and bring Islamist rule to nations like Afghanistan. They backed the Afghan rebels by funneling arms and Islamist Arab fighters into Afghanistan. One of those foreign militants was the son of a wealthy Saudi Arabian family, Osama bin Laden.

Afghanistan was already one of the world's poorest countries before the Soviet invasion. Conditions were only made worse by the Soviet occupation, which turned into a ten-year siege. More than one hundred thousand Afghans were killed. The

Soviet tanks take up positions in front of the Darulaman Palace in Kabul. The Soviets planned their invasion to be quick and decisive, however, it turned into a ten year siege.

combination of relentless bombing, land mines, and bulldozing destroyed Afghan agriculture and heavily damaged the country-side.

Ultimately, some 4.5 million Afghans—nearly a third of Afghanistan's prewar population—would leave the country between 1978 and 2001. Most of the refugees settled in camps across the border in Pakistan and Iran. Communities of exiled and expatriate Afghans sprang up elsewhere in Pakistan, in the United States and Canada, and around the exiled king in Rome. The fighting that started with the Soviet invasion also displaced up to 3 million more Afghans within the country, mostly poor rural villagers who could not afford to get out.

A New Sense of Duty

When Karzai's father and uncle were released from prison in late 1979, they became exiles too. The two men joined the anti-Soviet resistance movement from their new bases in Quetta and Peshawar, Pakistan. Filled with a new sense of patriotism, Karzai made up his mind to work with them there as soon as he finished his education.

An important factor in Karzai's decision was his renewed loyalty to his Pashtun tribe. Karzai's father's arrest and the Soviet invasion made him realize how much he valued his Afghan roots: "I suddenly realized how spoiled I was. … I realized that I had been consciously rejecting all the things that were really important and now were lost." He says his duty became clear during a

Afghan refugees coming from the Chaman border ride on top of a truck. Between 1978 and 2001 over four million Afghans would leave war-torn Afghanistan.

1980 visit to a refugee camp near his father's new home in Quetta. As soon as he arrived at the camp, he was rushed by hundreds of smiling Popolzai tribesmen:

> They thought that just because I was the khan's son, I had the power to help them. I felt ashamed, because I knew I was just a naive student who was spending his college years thinking only of himself and his ambition. I was not what they thought I was. My goal from that moment on was to become the man that those refugees thought I was. To become a man like my father.[25]

The Karzai Family: New Roots in the United States

The Karzai siblings were among the millions who fled the ongoing turmoil in Afghanistan. Karzai's brother Mahmoud had immigrated to the United States in 1976. By the early 1980s, his sister and all of his brothers, except Hamid, took advantage of American offers of asylum and followed him there.

In the United States, the Karzais finished their education and started careers. They launched a successful chain of Afghan restaurants called Helmand, named after Afghanistan's longest river. Abdul Ahmed became an engineer at the University of Maryland. Qayum earned a master's degree in political science at American University, then operated a Helmand branch in Baltimore. Mahmoud ran Helmand restaurants in San Francisco, Boston, and Cambridge, Massachusetts. Fouzia managed the branches in Massachusetts, and Ahmed Wali managed another branch in Chicago. Shah Wali became an engineer, and Abdul Wali became an assistant professor of biochemistry at the State University of New York at Stony Brook. Five of the siblings became naturalized U.S. citizens.

Karzai's first priority, however, was to complete his studies. He returned to Himachal Pradesh University and earned his master's degree in international relations and political science in 1982.

From India to Pakistan

In January 1983, the twenty-five-year-old Karzai joined his father in Quetta, Pakistan, and actively joined the Afghan resistance movement. Karzai became the spokesperson for the Afghan National Liberation Front (ANLF). The ANLF was one of seven major mujahideen groups struggling to push the Soviets out of Afghanistan. Unlike the radical Islamist groups that preached religious extremism and hatred of the West, the moderate ANLF was friendly to the United States and other Western powers. Karzai himself was disturbed by the growing strain of Islamic extremism among the mujahideen groups. He rejected radical Islam and terrorism because he believed extremism could only divide Afghans instead of restoring the stability Afghans had known under the monarchy. His sympathies lay with the ANLF and other groups who wanted to bring back the exiled king, Zahir Shah, and Afghans' traditional way of life.

Karzai was supported by his siblings, now all living in the United States, who sent profits from a family restaurant business to fund his resistance activities. Karzai worked from ANLF offices in Quetta and Peshawar; between the two cities, the Karzais kept at least three houses that also served as safe houses for resistance fighters. Karzai spent the rest of the 1980s drumming up military and financial support for the mujahideen, for example as a high-level go-between for the American Central Intelligence Agency (CIA) and mujahideen commanders.

The charming, well-dressed Karzai was known and liked in the community of foreign journalists, intelligence agents, aid workers, and Afghan refugees that filled Peshawar during the Soviet occupation. According to Mills:

> [Karzai] enjoyed mingling with the Western crowd. He would turn up at parties hosted by the director of the American

Center or the U.S. consul, drinking tea or soda and chatting easily with wine-swilling guests. He also liked to slip into Peshawar's only luxury hotel, the Intercontinental, for a dip in the swimming pool. I once told a gathering of South Asia analysts that while they may have thought of themselves as Afghan "experts," I was the only person in the room who had seen Hamid Karzai in a Speedo.[26]

Karzai was not yet viewed as a potential Afghan leader because he had no military or battle experience. To many tribal Afghans, directly confronting the enemy was the true test of leadership.

The Soviets Go Home

Despite their enemy's many advantages, the fierce mujahideen managed to fight the Soviets to a standstill. The rebels' guerrilla tactics—sabotage and endless rocket attacks—slowly sapped Soviet military strength and morale. The longer the war dragged on, the more unpopular it was with the Soviet people. The Soviet Union wanted to control Afghanistan to exploit its mineral resources and use the country as a base of trade and military operations. By 1986, however, the Soviets were looking for a new Afghan Communist president, someone brutal enough to control the rebellion so they could quietly give up. They found him in Muhammad Najibullah, the head of the Afghan secret police. In 1987 the Soviets announced a gradual military withdrawal, and on February 15, 1989, the last Soviet military units crossed the border in defeat.

Karzai had always predicted victory: "No occupation force can stay in Afghanistan against the will of the Afghan people. None ever has, none ever will." He adds bitterly, "What we did not predict was the disaster that followed."[27]

The mujahideen thought they would be able to ride triumphantly into Kabul as soon as the Soviet tanks withdrew. They were wrong. Najibullah managed to stay in power for three years after the last Russian troops left the country. He held on partly because the mujahideen were not a united front. Their leaders

Soviet troops leave Afghanistan, nine years after they invaded the country. Approximately one million Afghans lost their lives during the occupation, while Soviet deaths were estimated at around fifteen thousand.

had little in common other than their shared goal of defeating the communists. These strongmen, or Afghan warlords, controlled their own private militias and made their own laws.

The Najibullah regime finally fell to the mujahideen in April 1992. Najibullah fled to the sanctuary of the UN compound in Kabul. He spent the next four years there under UN protection. Meanwhile, the once-mighty Soviet Union had collapsed in 1991. Once the American government no longer viewed the communists as a threat, it stopped sending arms shipments to the mujahideen and lost interest in Afghan politics. Afghanistan was on its own now.

Civil War

The first mujahideen force to ride into Kabul after Najibullah fled was led by the ethnic Tajik Islamic scholar Burhanuddin Rabbani. Rival mujahideen militias and criminal gangs rushed in after him. Pockets of communist Afghan army forces were still defending the capital, and the takeover was bloody. An estimated seventy thousand Afghan civilians were killed. Kabul suffered major destruction. There was widespread looting of homes, stores, and museums. Before long, the mujahideen were fighting each other as well as the communists.

The leaders of the rival rebel factions tried to avoid all-out civil war by reluctantly agreeing to form a coalition government, with Rabbani as president. Hoping this power-sharing agreement would stabilize the nation, Karzai returned to Kabul from exile. Because he was fluent in several languages and had many contacts among the international news, intelligence, and aid communities, he was offered a post as Rabbani's deputy foreign minister. He spent most of his time in that job trying to get the coalition partners to cooperate with each other.

Karzai's efforts failed. The coalition was hopelessly split. On one side were moderates such as Karzai who wanted to restore an independent, traditional Afghanistan, headed by a king. Arrayed against them were militant groups of radical Islamists who wanted to impose their views on the Afghan people and allow shadowy foreign partners to influence Afghan affairs.

The coalition soon fell apart, and civil war broke out in full force. According to Rubin, the mujahideen groups that had managed to work together to drive out the communists spent the four chaotic years of Rabbani's rule "rocketing one another and Kabul to smithereens."[28] With no hope for a stable government, Karzai fled the country in 1994 and made his way back to safety in Pakistan.

The Rise of the Taliban

Karzai returned to Pakistan just as a new mujahideen movement was emerging. Its foot soldiers came from the madrassas, or Islamic schools, in refugee camps along the Pakistan border and in Kandahar. They called themselves the Taliban, meaning "the students." They preached peace, unity, and above all, law and order with swift sharia justice. War-weary Afghans thought Taliban rule was their best hope for peace.

Karzai was one of those early Taliban supporters. He knew some of the mullahs who founded the movement. They too were ethnic Pashtuns from Kandahar, whom he describes as "very fine people. ... The U.S. supported them. The UN supported them, and they were good people."[29] In 1994 Karzai became the Taliban's chief fund-raiser. From his base in Pakistan, he channeled both foreign funds and his own money to the movement.

The Taliban takeover was amazingly quick for two reasons. First, the Afghan people welcomed them. Poor Afghans who had been victimized for so long believed the warlords and other criminals would be swiftly brought to justice by the Taliban. Second, some mujahideen warlords simply decided the Taliban were unstoppable and let them have their way.

Students of the Jamia Salfia Madrasa reading the Koran. The Taliban come from schools such as this one, in particular from those in refugee camps along the Afghan-Pakistan border.

By then the Taliban-Karzai connection had broken down. Karzai began to suspect something was very wrong with the movement in 1995. When he became critical, his Taliban contacts stopped calling. By the time Kabul fell to the Taliban in 1996, he says,

> they were taken over by foreigners, by the Pakistanis, by the Arab elements, by radical Muslims, radical extremist elements from all over the world, and terrorists mixed up with them. So the movement was completely sabotaged. The good ones in it were somehow sidelined or assassinated or made to sit at home, and the bad ones kept rising and rising and rising. That's how this movement ... that could have been one that could bring peace turned into a killing machine, turned into an instrument of terror and torture for Afghans.[30]

A Modern-Day Inquisition

Once in control, the Taliban proclaimed a new Afghan state, the Islamic Emirate of Afghanistan. Its emir, or leader, was Taliban commander Muhammad Omar, known as Mullah Omar, who ran the country from his base in Kandahar. Under Mullah Omar, the Taliban preached an extreme brand of Wahhabi Islam, with the strictest enforcement of sharia ever seen in the Muslim world. Soon the regime was being compared to the medieval Inquisition.

The Taliban's idea of swift justice for the former communist president Najibullah, still hiding out at the UN compound, was a grisly sign of things to come. British journalist Christina Lamb reports that when the Taliban took over, "they took [Najibullah] back to the Arg, castrated him in his former bedroom, tied him to a Toyota Land Cruiser and dragged him round the grounds before hanging him from a traffic island."[31]

Afghan women were banned from holding jobs, attending school, or appearing in public unless they were completely covered by a cloak-like burka. Newspapers, music, and textbooks

Under the Taliban regime, women were not allowed to study or work. Women were also forced to wear a traditional burka, that covers them from head to toe.

that were not approved by the Taliban and were also banned. Dissent and protest were not tolerated. Brutal punishments included public executions in Kabul's Ghazi Stadium.

Under the Taliban, Afghan farmers were pressured to abandon other crops and grow the opium poppy, the plant used to make heroin and other illegal narcotics, because drugs were more profitable than food. Cultivation of poppy and manufacture and export of drugs was soon the biggest share of the Afghan economy. In an even more sinister development, the Taliban formed alliances with foreign terrorist organizations and let them establish more than one hundred terrorist training camps in Afghanistan. The most famous site was Tarnak Farms in Kandahar, the camp of Osama bin Laden and his al Qaeda organization.

Warnings and Reprisals

From Quetta, Karzai began to campaign against the Taliban and work to reinstate the former king, Zahir Shah. He made weekly visits to U.S., British, German, and Italian embassies in Pakistan. He also traveled to Washington, D.C., and European capitals to warn officials in person that the Taliban and their terrorist partners posed a terrible threat, not just to Afghanistan but to the entire world. His warnings mostly fell on deaf ears. As an official with the British Foreign Office admits, "We used to say, 'It's that Karzai fellow again,' and try to palm him off with someone junior."[32]

Karzai's and his father's anti-Taliban activities made them targets of the extremists. On July 14, 1999, Abdul Ahad Karzai was assassinated, shot in the back by unknown gunmen as he returned from evening prayers at a mosque in Quetta. Karzai believes the assassins were either members of the Taliban or their backers, Pakistani Inter-Services Intelligence (ISI) agents.

In a courageous move, Karzai decided to return his father's body to Kandahar for burial. He led the funeral convoy himself. Karzai was as much an enemy of the Taliban as his father was; by entering the Taliban stronghold he risked being killed too. But something stopped the Taliban from attacking the mourners. Perhaps it was the Pashtun code of honoring a brave enemy, even after murdering him. Perhaps the Taliban did not want to risk inciting a tribal uprising by harming the dead khan's son. In a dramatic and somber scene, the armed Taliban stood aside and allowed the unarmed Karzai to bring his father home to Kandahar.

Respect for a Murdered Enemy: The Karzai Funeral Convoy

Karzai's bold decision to bury his father in his ancestral village of Karz was a key moment in his rise to leader of the anti-Taliban resistance. He put himself at great risk when he organized a huge funeral procession to carry Abdul Ahad's remains from Quetta into the Taliban enemy stronghold of Kandahar. Karzai himself led the convoy of up to three hundred vehicles on the 124-mile journey (200km). Not a hand was raised against Karzai or the other mourners. He describes the dramatic event:

> Lots of people came to me and said, "Don't do that. You will go into Afghanistan and the Taliban will arrest you." I said, "No. I want to go, and if they have the guts, let them arrest me." ... It was so risky. ... We had no guns, we had no arms, we had nothing. We just moved in. But of course the Taliban were [intimidated by this show of defiance.] They took all the city corners and crossroads and protected them with tanks.

Quoted in Academy of Achievement, "Hamid Karzai Interview," June 2, 2002. Revised October 9, 2006. www.achievement.org/autodoc/page/kar0int-1.

The New Khan

Traditionally, the title of tribal chief is passed down to the eldest son in a family, but all of Karzai's older brothers were living in the United States. Moreover, Karzai had demonstrated leadership potential by defiantly and successfully leading his father's funeral convoy from Quetta back to Kandahar. Karzai's direct challenge to the enemy impressed Afghan tribal elders more than his diplomatic contacts ever did. Soon after Abdul Ahad Karzai

Zeenat Quraishi Karzai

Most Afghans are unaware that Hamid Karzai has been married since 1999. Zeenat Quraishi Karzai was a Pashtun physician working as an obstetrician/gynecologist in the Afghan refugee camps in Pakistan before their arranged marriage. As Karzai's wife and first lady of Afghanistan, however, she has assumed the conservative Pashtun woman's traditional role and stays out of sight with the couple's only child, a son named Mirwais (meaning "light of the house"), born on January 25, 2007.

Karzai has been criticized for supporting Afghan women's civil rights in words but oppressing his own wife under tight security. Dr. Zeenat, as she is known in the Arg, gives rare interviews only to female journalists, with no cameras or tape recorders allowed. Except at a state visit from President George W. Bush and First Lady Laura Bush in 2005, she has not appeared in public. In a 2004 *Telegraph* interview, she claimed, "This is the life I have chosen. I want to be in Afghanistan, and never want to leave." In 2009, however, she reportedly complained that she could not go out without Karzai's permission, and she once told a reporter, "I want to travel around the world, I have heard great things about Europe but have never been there."

Quoted in Hamida Ghafour, "Afghan First Lady's Quiet Public Debut," *Telegraph*, April 12, 2004. www.telegraph.co.uk/news/worldnews/asia/afghanistan/1458985/Afghan-First-Ladys-quiet-public-debut.html.

Quoted in Sahil, Jamali4U Forum, October 24, 2009. http://forum.jamali4u.com/index.php?topic=4131.0.

Zeenat Karzai, wife of Afghan President Hamid Karzai, makes a rare public appearance to take part in a ceremony marking International Women's Day.

was buried, a council of Popolzai elders named Hamid Karzai the new khan of their clan.

The Popolzai elders also told him his bachelor days were over. Now forty-one years old, Karzai had spent more time on his political struggles than on his personal life. He had reportedly been close to an American *Wall Street Journal* reporter who was working in Afghanistan. Nonetheless, he was an obedient Pashtun who understood that a Pashtun khan's marrying an American woman would be unacceptable. By the end of 1999, in an arranged marriage, Karzai and his distant cousin Zeenat Quraishi, a Pashtun physician from his own tribe, were married.

Karzai had earned the traditional Afghan leadership role. The old Afghanistan was in ruins, however, and there was no place under the Taliban for him to exercise his new authority. He rejoined the resistance in Pakistan, unaware that in two years he would be catapulted from tribal leader to national leader.

Chapter 3

Driving Out the Taliban

The September 11, 2001 terrorist attacks on the United States suddenly focused the world's attention on Afghanistan. Just as suddenly, the spotlight fell on Hamid Karzai. His entrance onto the world stage required a combination of leadership skills: good communication, the ability to inspire trust, and a flair for self-promotion.

Anti-Taliban Resistance

Afghanistan under the Taliban was considered a rogue state by the international community. The only nations that officially recognized the Taliban regime of 1996–2001 were Pakistan, Saudi Arabia, and the United Arab Emirates. As Taliban human rights abuses mounted, opposition to the regime grew, both within and outside the country.

The most important anti-Taliban force within the country was the Northern Alliance, another temporary alliance in the ongoing turmoil. Just as rival mujahideen groups had managed to unite from 1979–1992 to drive out the Soviets and Afghan Communists, so did rival politicians and warlords unite as the Northern Alliance from 1996–2001 to defeat their common Taliban enemy. The insurgents who formed the Northern Alliance were mostly ethnic Tajiks and Uzbeks from the north. Despite the title, however, the alliance included rebels from all over the country. The best-known Northern Alliance politician was former president Rabbani. The most respected and powerful Northern Alliance military leader was Ahmad Shah Massoud, famously known as "the lion of Panjshir," in his home province. Massoud, a moderate Tajik, was a hero of the mujahideen war against the Soviets in the 1980s.

After his father's funeral in 1999, Karzai returned to his anti-Taliban activities in Pakistan. He still had trouble getting Western government officials to listen to his urgent warnings about Taliban sponsorship of international terrorism. According to a London *Sunday Times* profile of Karzai, "For several years he was dismissed as a 'coffee shop' politician who kept a salon in the Pakistani border town of Quetta at which malcontents drank green tea, munched sugared almonds, muttered and did nothing more."[33]

After the murder of his father, however, Karzai took his battle to oust the Taliban to the media, and his voice got louder. He gave interviews to the BBC and the U.S. news and information service Voice of America. He smuggled anti-Taliban pamphlets into Afghanistan. He communicated frequently with Massoud of the Northern Alliance about Karzai's plan to incite a Pashtun uprising against the Taliban in the south. He tirelessly delivered his message—that shadowy foreign extremists were using Afghanistan as a base of terrorist operations—to anyone who would listen.

The Karzai brothers began to play a bigger role in the resistance, too. Ahmed Wali stayed on in Quetta with Hamid after their father's funeral and coordinated deals between anti-Taliban leaders. Back in the United States, Qayum got busy lobbying U.S. officials for support and founded the nonprofit Afghans for a Civil Society. Meanwhile, CIA paramilitary teams were covertly active in Afghanistan in the late 1990s. However, they were there not to bring down the Taliban, but to capture or kill Bin Laden, who was wanted for 1998 attacks on U.S. embassies in Africa.

The World Finally Pays Attention

All at once, in the late summer of 2001, things came to a head for Karzai in Quetta. First, the Pakistani government, which supported Mullah Omar and the Taliban regime, refused to renew his visa

Flames spew out of the two World Trade Center towers after they are struck by two commercial airlines in a terrorist attack on September 11, 2001, in New York City. The towers, a city landmark for 25 years, later both collapsed.

and ordered Karzai to leave the country by the end of September. On September 9, Northern Alliance commander Massoud was assassinated by al Qaeda suicide bombers. Osama bin Laden had ordered the assassination as a favor to his Taliban protectors.

Two days later, Karzai's worst fear—that ignoring the threat of Islamic extremists in Afghanistan would lead to a catastrophic attack—was realized. On September 11, 2001, terrorist attacks on New York City and Washington, D.C., killed nearly three thousand people. The terrorists who crashed commercial airplanes into the World Trade Center, the Pentagon, and a Pennsylvania field were al Qaeda operatives who had trained in Afghanistan under Bin Laden.

Karzai was in Islamabad, Pakistan, on September 11, making his usual rounds of the embassies. When he heard the terrible news, he canceled the rest of his appointments. "After all," he says, "there would be no point in reminding them of what I had been telling them for six years."[34]

U.S. president George W. Bush demanded that the Taliban hand over Bin Laden and all other terrorists on Afghan soil and close the terrorist training camps. Taliban leaders refused, perhaps because they were indebted to Bin Laden for assassinating Massoud. They allowed him and his men to flee to mountain caves in rugged border regions. Bush reacted with three main efforts: an immediate, international military response in Afghanistan; a broader war on international terrorism; and an investigation into why U.S. intelligence agencies failed to prevent the September 11 attack. The military response was quick: On October 7, a U.S.- and UK-led coalition, code-named Operation Enduring Freedom, launched an aerial bombing campaign on the Taliban. It was the first stage in the U.S. war in Afghanistan.

Karzai in Battle

Meanwhile, Karzai boldly set out to jump-start the tribal uprising he had been planning in Kandahar. He knew from his CIA contacts that the coalition bombing campaign was about to begin and that the U.S. military was looking for on-the-ground support

The Coalition

The international coalition that Karzai began working with in 2001 is actually a mix of three operations. The U.S.-led operation is code-named Operation Enduring Freedom. The British operation is code-named Operation Herrick. The third operation is the International Security Assistance Force (ISAF). This forty-six-country force was created by the UN but is now under the control of one of the world's major military alliances, the North Atlantic Treaty Organization (NATO). In the war in Afghanistan, some countries deploy troops in both Operation Enduring Freedom and the ISAF. The United States, for example, is by far the largest force in both operations. A general reference to "the coalition" could mean troops assigned to any one of these operations.

from Afghan civilians. Expelled from Pakistan, Karzai decided to sneak into southern Afghanistan and try to rally that support himself. He had assurances from American contacts in Quetta that U.S. forces would back him up once he was inside.

Karzai made his move in early October, just as the U.S. bombing campaign began. After a last-minute farewell to his wife, Karzai and a couple of friends secretly crossed the border on two motorbikes. Disguised in rough clothing and a turban, he was armed only with a little money and a CIA satellite phone.

For more than two weeks, Karzai says, he moved from one safe house to another in his home province of Kandahar, gathering nervous supporters. His growing group moved north into the mountains, mostly on foot, dodging coalition bombing raids and bribing their way through Taliban checkpoints. He met with tribal elders and mullahs along the way. All were sympathetic, but no one was willing to challenge the Taliban without weapons. Karzai called for a U.S. weapons drop, which was parachuted in just in time for Karzai and his vastly outnumbered band of 150 men to fight off a day-long Taliban attack.

In the midst of the firefight, Karzai says, he decided to issue a nationwide call to arms via his satellite phone. He got through to a BBC station and convinced a staffer to put him on the air with dire words: "Don't you hear the gunfire? Can't you hear the bullets? … We want to make this call. Please don't kill this moment for Afghanistan."[35] Then he put his spokesman on the line, whose words were broadcast by BBC radio across the country: "I am speaking for Karzai. We declare a loya jirga [the traditional national Afghan grand council] against the Taliban. This is a national uprising against them."[36] Then the batteries went dead.

Karzai's band of rebels went on to win the firefight. The Taliban attackers scattered. Instead of admitting defeat, however, they spread the rumor that Karzai had stopped communicating not because his satellite phone had died but because he had been killed. This turned out to be a mistake, because it angered Afghans and inspired them to join the uprising. The growing tribal rebellion in the south ended up hastening the Taliban's defeat.

Legend and Truth

Karzai is a born storyteller, and he enjoys relating this dramatic adventure. It also benefits Karzai to be seen as a national hero, and he is willing to fudge the facts if that boosts his heroic image. Other accounts of Karzai's story dispute his version. Rubin writes, for example, that Karzai's dramatic BBC call to arms was not made in the thick of battle: "Karzai and the men he gathered were chased by the Taliban but fought them off, [then called Karzai's CIA contact for help]. Navy Seals landed, pulled Karzai and tribal leaders out and flew them to a base in Pakistan. … [Then] live on the BBC, he insisted he was [speaking from the front lines] somewhere in Afghanistan."[37]

Although it was embellished, Karzai's story served the purpose of cementing his authority among the southern tribes, for whom bravery in battle is a traditional test of leadership. His bravery in going into the Taliban stronghold is undeniable. His plan worked: The Afghan people did rise against the Taliban, and the regime fell.

Everyone's Man at the Bonn Conference

Operation Enduring Freedom was not a complete success. Taliban supreme leader Mullah Omar went into hiding, and Bin Laden escaped capture. One important goal was achieved: On December 5, 2001, only two months after the war began, the Taliban signed an unconditional surrender.

Wanted poster distributed by the FBI which places Osama bin Laden on the FBI's Ten Most Wanted list. After September 11, 2001 the Taliban allowed Bin Laden to escape to mountain caves along the border.

FBI TEN MOST WANTED FUGITIVE

MURDER OF U.S. NATIONALS OUTSIDE THE UNITED STATES;
CONSPIRACY TO MURDER U.S. NATIONALS OUTSIDE THE UNITED STATES;
ATTACK ON A FEDERAL FACILITY RESULTING IN DEATH

USAMA BIN LADEN

Date of Photograph Unknown

Aliases: Usama Bin Muhammad Bin Ladin, Shaykh Usama Bin Ladin, the Prince, the Emir, Abu Abdallah, Mujahid Shaykh, Hajj, the Director

DESCRIPTION

Date of Birth:	1957	Hair:	Brown
Place of Birth:	Saudi Arabia	Eyes:	Brown
Height:	6' 4" to 6' 6"	Complexion:	Olive
Weight:	Approximately 160 pounds	Sex:	Male
Build:	Thin	Nationality:	Saudi Arabian
Occupation(s):	Unknown		
Remarks:	He is the leader of a terrorist organization known as Al-Qaeda "The Base." He walks with a cane.		

CAUTION

USAMA BIN LADEN IS WANTED IN CONNECTION WITH THE AUGUST 7, 1998, BOMBINGS OF THE UNITED STATES EMBASSIES IN DAR ES SALAAM, TANZANIA AND NAIROBI, KENYA. THESE ATTACKS KILLED OVER 200 PEOPLE.

CONSIDERED ARMED AND EXTREMELY DANGEROUS

IF YOU HAVE ANY INFORMATION CONCERNING THIS PERSON, PLEASE CONTACT YOUR LOCAL FBI OFFICE OR THE NEAREST U.S. EMBASSY OR CONSULATE.

REWARD

The United States Government is offering a reward of up to $5 million for information leading directly to the apprehension or conviction of Usama Bin Laden.

The surrender was part of an agreement hammered out at the International Conference on Afghanistan in Bonn, Germany. Once military victory was declared, coalition partners organized the conference to figure out a timetable for a new Afghan government. The delegates included leading Afghan exiles, representatives of the Northern Alliance, and a variety of Western political and military officials. The agreement created a temporary government, the Afghan Transitional Authority (ATA). The man selected for a six-month term as interim chair of the ATA was Hamid Karzai.

Karzai seemed the perfect choice. To each stakeholder in Afghanistan's future, Karzai offered something to identify with. To the delegates at the Bonn Conference, he was part freedom fighter, part aristocrat. To Afghan religious conservatives, he was a devout Muslim who never drank alcohol and prayed five times a day. To tribal Afghan society, he was a Pashtun khan. To the anti-Taliban resistance, he was a war hero. To U.S. and British military and political leaders, he was a pro-Western, well-educated Afghan who could speak English. Even the Northern Alliance warlords, who really wanted to fill the power vacuum themselves, endorsed Karzai because they knew he believed in Afghan unity and would bring them into his government. With their shady reputations as thugs during the civil war, they knew they could not get there on their own.

Karzai was still in rural Kandahar when he got the news. He flew to Kabul, where he was met by the Tajik Northern Alliance commander Muhammad Qasim Fahim and one hundred of his soldiers. Fahim was astonished to see Karzai arrive with no bodyguards or personal militia, no weapons, and no caravan of armored SUVs. When he asked Karzai where all his men were, Karzai the unifier replied, "You are my men. ... All of you who are Afghans are my men."[38] The Northern Alliance tribes had put their faith in a southern Pashtun; now he was putting his faith in them.

In an emotional and dignified ceremony in December 2001, Karzai was officially named interim chair of the ATA. In perhaps the most moving moment of the ceremony, the Russian representative approached Karzai, shook his hand, and said he was very sorry for what the Soviet Union had done to Afghanistan from 1979 to 1989, the first and most destructive period of Afghanistan's long era of war.

The 2002 Loya Jirga

In June 2002, the end of the six-month term, the Karzai administration organized and oversaw a Loya Jirga in the capital. About two thousand delegates representing Afghan regions, political groups, and religious factions met at Kabul Polytechnic University. It was a rather chaotic gathering with lots of debate and deal making, but it resulted in a plan for a democratic Afghanistan.

Loya jirga (grand council) delegates attend their meeting in Kabul, Afghanistan, Friday, June 14, 2002. The Loya Jirga is based on an Afghan tradition whose purpose is to bring far-flung community leaders together for important decisions in times of need.

The Loya Jirga: Afghanistan's National Grand Council

The tradition of jirgas, meetings of male village elders to settle tribal disputes, is as old as Afghanistan. Since the 1700s, the jirga has also been practiced on a national scale as a grand council meeting of tribal leaders called a Loya Jirga, the tribal equivalent of a parliament or an emergency session of the UN General Assembly. According to the website Afghanland.com, there are two types of Loya Jirga. One is convened by Afghan citizens at a time of crisis when decisions must be made about war, elections, and national sovereignty. The other is convened by the Afghan ruler when he needs to consult with his people on important national issues. Karzai called for the first kind of Loya Jirga in his dramatic BBC radio call in 2001. He called for the second kind in 2002, when Afghans came together to form an interim government.

The council appointed Karzai to serve a two-year term as head of the ATA. Under interim president Karzai, the ATA was to draft and adopt a constitution for a new, representative Afghan state and hold democratic elections for a president and legislature. In more general terms, U.S. backers made Karzai's job clear: spread democracy; secure the country and fight terrorism; and rebuild Afghanistan's infrastructure, social services, and economy.

Karzai would have plenty of input from others on these tasks. All the jockeying for influence at the Loya Jirga resulted in the additional appointments of three deputy presidents, a special security advisor, twenty-seven ministers of various departments, and one supreme court justice. Key among them were Fahim, as defense minister and deputy president, and Abdullah Abdullah as foreign minister. Abdullah was a well-educated, English-speaking former ophthalmologist who was respected as honest and disciplined by Western diplomats.

Optimism and Signs of Recovery

The next two years were a sort of honeymoon for the popular Karzai. He and his wife moved into the Arg Palace, an 80-acre walled compound (32ha) in Kabul. Inside the walls were large office buildings, a mosque, and the grand houses that were royal residences during the monarchy period. Although most of Kabul had been destroyed in the civil war, the Arg was still intact. The Karzai residence and the Gul Khana (the president's office building) had only minimal damage.

Karzai set out to give the Afghan people a sense of stability. In 2002 he brought the elderly Zahir Shah back from exile and bestowed on him the title of "Father of the Nation." The former king lived in comfortable quarters in the Arg among friends and family until his death in 2007 at the age of ninety-two. Karzai also boosted national pride by announcing that Afghanistan's greatest national treasure, the Bactrian Hoard, was safe in Afghan hands.

President Hamid Karzai (left) and Afghanistan's former King Mohammad Zahir Shah meet at the palace November 3, 2002, in Kabul, Afghanistan. The two inaugurated a special committee set up to draft a new constitution for the war ravaged nation.

This two-thousand-year-old collection of over twenty thousand objects made of gold and gemstones had gone missing during the decades of war.

With UN assistance, more than sixty-three thousand former fighters surrendered their weapons to the ministry of defense. Trained teams began the dangerous process of clearing hundreds of thousands of land mines, starting with the major cities and airports. Feeling safer, Afghans reopened their shops. A bonanza of consumer goods soon appeared in the markets, such as cell phones, pirated CDs and DVDs, and household appliances. These goods, and Afghans' hunger for news from the outside world, created a huge demand for communication networks and electricity, both of which Karzai promised to restore.

The reconstruction and reopening of Karzai's old school, Habibia High School in Kabul, reflected Afghans' new sense of freedom. So many students showed up for classes that tents were used for classrooms and students went to school in shifts. Another sign of expanded civil rights was the 2003 constitutional convention's decision to guarantee women 25 percent of the seats in parliament. In general, public spirits (and expectations) were high.

From 2002 to 2004, Karzai also spent a lot of time traveling to Western capitals seeking foreign aid and investment. Always a good fund-raiser, his speeches usually reminded audiences of the interconnectedness of the world and the dangers of ignoring poor countries like Afghanistan.

Karzai's Personal Style

To the international media, Karzai was a new star. His popularity was enhanced by his personal charisma and refined manners. He also had style that made foreigners take notice. Journalist Jon Lee Anderson writes that "Pashtun men, Kandaharis in particular, are very conscious of their personal appearance. Many of them line their eyes with black kohl and color their toenails, and sometimes their fingernails, with henna. Some also dye their hair. It is quite common to see otherwise sober-seeming older men with long

Hamid Karzai wears his karacul hat as he arrives at a ceremony marking the start of the school year. The karacul became very popular in Kabul.

beards that are a flaming, almost punk-like orange color."[39]

Karzai is a Pashtun from Kandahar, and he is very conscious of his personal appearance, but he does not go that far. He is a lean, broad-shouldered man about 5 feet 10 inches tall (177.8cm). Bald and olive-skinned, he has a hawklike nose and warm but penetrating eyes. In exile in Pakistan in the 1980s, he was clean shaven and wore conservative Western clothes—slacks and a blazer, jeans and a leather jacket. In Afghanistan in 2001, early in Operation Enduring Freedom, a photograph of Karzai with U.S. Special Forces shows him draped in a plain Afghan shawl, with a full beard and a turban.

Karzai stepped into the international spotlight with considerably more polish. In 2002, silver beard neatly trimmed, he started appearing in an Afghan *chapan*, a long-sleeved silk overcoat of jewel-colored stripes—purple, green, turquoise—with intricate threading in gold or white. He wore a *chapan* or an elegant cape over a collarless Nehru shirt, loose trousers, and a vest. Instead of a turban or a *pakul* (the common soft wool hat with a rolled brim and flat top adopted by the mujahideen), Karzai wore a karakul hat. This peaked lamb's wool cap made Karzai instantly recognizable around the world. His unique wardrobe led Gucci

"The Chicest Man on the Planet"?

When Karzai became interim leader and then president of Afghanistan, his trademark karakul hat became the height of fashion, not just in Kabul but also in Paris and Milan. Afghan men paid up to three thousand dollars for a karakul hat to replace the black turbans and white skullcaps of the Taliban. Karzai himself purchased dozens from the hat shops in Mazar-i-Sharif. The peaked cap is made of the rippled, velvety-soft pelt of fetal karakul sheep, better known in English as Persian lamb. A full pelt is needed to make each hat. The lambskin is sewn into a tube, stretched over a head-shaped wooden form, and pounded into shape with stones.

The hat's popularity, however, has fallen along with the president's. In 2010 *New York Times* reporter Rod Nordland wrote that

> young men no longer wear it. ... All but 12 of the [hat] shops have closed. ... Those remaining say they are lucky to sell a hat a day. "I went back to my village in Logar wearing my karakul hat," said Ahmed, an Afghan in his 50s, who was shopping for a new hat, "and people laughed: 'There goes the old man who thinks he's president.'"

Rod Nordland, "The Afghan Leaders' Hat, Always More than Just Headgear, Is Losing Its Cachet," *New York Times*, January 26, 2010. www.nytimes.com/2010/01/27/world/asia/27karzai.html.

fashion designer Tom Ford to dub Karzai "the chicest man on the planet"[40] in January 2002.

Striking as Karzai's signature look is, it is not the way an Afghan really dresses. Karzai's outfits are inventions that reflect his goal of representing all Afghans. As Anderson explains:

> Westerners often assume that [Karzai's] elaborate outfits are the traditional dress of his people, the Pashtuns. In fact, Karzai assembles them as [tributes] to Afghanistan's disparate ethnic

groups—they are costumes, roughly akin to the baseball caps that an American politician might wear while campaigning in different parts of the country. The striped green silk *chapan* cape … is Uzbek; the gray karakul hat he often wears is traditionally Tajik.[41]

"The World Will Forget About Us Now"

Inside and outside of Afghanistan, it seemed Karzai could do no wrong. Then in 2003, the United States invaded Iraq. Once the Taliban were no longer a threat, only six thousand Western peacekeeping troops remained in Afghanistan, all in Kabul. America was still the country's biggest financial donor: Some $10.4 billion in pledges, one-third of all development aid to Afghanistan, was expected from the United States in addition to billions of dollars of military aid. A worried Karzai remembered that the Americans had lost interest in Afghanistan twelve years earlier, once the Soviets were no longer a threat. He predicted that the U.S. war in Iraq meant "the world will forget about us now."[42] He turned out to be right.

Chapter 4

President Karzai

In a historic election, Karzai became president of Afghanistan in 2004. With the United States distracted by the war in Iraq, however, the job of rebuilding his country proved much harder than he imagined. It seemed President Karzai's every attempt to be a strong leader backfired.

Afghanistan's First Democratic Presidential Election

The first nationwide democratic elections in Afghan history took place in November 2004. Some 8 million Afghans, 40 percent of them women, went to the polls. Karzai won 55 percent of the vote for president against seventeen opponents. He purposely ran as an independent to make it clear to voters that he wanted to represent all Afghans, not a narrow party. On December 7, 2004, Karzai took office for a five-year term as His Excellency Hamid Karzai, President of the Islamic Republic of Afghanistan.

In his campaign, Karzai promised the Afghan people his administration would provide basic services. He promised to improve literacy and the status of women. He said he would clamp down on the drug trade and deal with the refugee problem in Pakistan.

Karzai also said he would secure the country against terrorism. To do that, he pledged to build a strong Afghan military: the Afghan National Army (ANA) and the Afghan National Army Air Force. (Afghanistan is a landlocked country and has no navy.)

Afghan President Hamid Karzai casts his ballot in Kabul in Afghanistan's first ever direct election Saturday, October 9, 2004.

Unity Through Buzkashi

Afghanistan celebrated Karzai's inauguration in 2004 as Afghans have celebrated for centuries: with a buzkashi tournament, a sort of headless goat polo that is the closest thing to a national sport. The competition begins by laying a disemboweled, headless goat carcass in an open field or stadium, surrounded by fifty or more men on horseback. Nick B. Mills offers this play-by-play of a sport that can go on for days:

> Clenching their short, brutal, wood-handled whips in their teeth when not beating their horse or someone else's, [the horsemen] try to maneuver their mounts into position over the dead goat, producing a wild scrum of plunging, whinnying, biting horses. In the midst of the madness, a rider will reach down ... grasp the seventy-five-pound carcass, lift it off the ground, and try to ride away with it, while other riders pursue and try to wrestle the carcass away. ... Such is the strength of the men that often a leg will be ripped from the carcass, leaving one rider victorious and the other holding a leg of goat.

Nick B. Mills, *Karzai: The Failing American Intervention and the Struggle for Afghanistan.* New York: Wiley, 2007, pp. 29–30.

Roadblocks to Progress

Karzai's agenda was ambitious. Unfortunately for the Afghan people, it was full of promises that Karzai found impossible to keep. Karzai had already been in power for two years, and the country was still a far cry from the picture-postcard Afghanistan of his childhood. Kabul was still in ruins. There were no good roads between cities. Open land all over the countryside was marked by pathways of white stones and chalk skull-and-crossbones indicating land mines. In the 1980s, the Soviets had bombed the country's vital irrigation canals—underground channels that carried water from the base of mountains to valley farms—to destroy mujahideen hideouts. The lack of irrigation followed by years of severe drought had dried up wells, farmland, and orchards and left the once-fertile countryside parched and dusty.

Improving education would be no easier. Among the millions of Afghans who had fled since the fighting began in 1979 were the country's intellectuals, liberals, and professionals—the educated class. Most of the Afghan women who stayed behind shrouded themselves in burkas when the Taliban was in power. Many still feared reprisals from powerful Islamic fundamentalists if they showed their faces. After twenty-five years of war, less than 13

Karzai's First Inaugural Address

On December 7, 2004, Karzai was sworn in as Afghanistan's first democratically elected president. In his inaugural address, Karzai delivered a pointed warning to an audience that included U.S. vice president Dick Cheney and three former U.S. presidents:

> I must hasten to say that our fight against terrorism is not yet over, even though we have succeeded to reduce this common enemy of humanity to a lesser threat in this country. The relationship between terrorism and narcotics and the continued threat of extremism in the region and the world at large are a source of continued concern. A decisive victory over terrorism requires serious and continued cooperation at regional and international levels.

Hamid Karzai, "H.E. Hamid Karzai's Inaugural Speech," Teracom Network Services, December 7, 2004. http://users.tns.net/~mroashan/politics/Documents/InauguralSpeechHEPresidentHamidKarzai.pdf.

percent of females and only 43 percent of males over the age of fifteen could read or write.

No one really had a solution for the drug problem, either. Under the Taliban, Afghanistan had become the world's biggest hashish producer and the supplier of 90 percent of the world's opium. Almost everyone in the south, where most of the opium poppy is grown, depended on poppy income, including top officials. According to reporter William Grimes: "In June 2005 police raided the mansion of Helmand's governor … and found nine metric tons of opium. [It was hard to believe the governor's explanation] that he had seized the opium from traffickers and was merely waiting for the appropriate moment to dispose of it."[43]

As if converting the poppy economy were not hard enough, Afghans were becoming addicted to heroin and opium in record numbers. During Karzai's first term, the number of Afghan opiate addicts doubled to more than 230,000 people, 3 percent of the adult population.

"Selling Brand Karzai"

Nevertheless, the U.S. and Afghan governments tried hard to project an image of progress that critic Marc W. Herold calls "selling Brand Karzai." In addition to fanfare over the 2004 election, Herold says, the mass media was full of optimistic images of "modern buildings sprouting up and new asphalt strips going off into the horizon … beauty salons are opening up, kids are flying kites, adults converse via cell phones, and the 'hideous' burka is on the way out."[44] These messages were not false, but they did mask the widespread hardship that still existed.

In his interviews, Karzai focused on more substantial signs of progress such as the opening of schools and maternity hospitals, new telephone systems, and the recent rains that helped farmers grow food after the long drought. Again and again he told Afghans that rebuilding was going to take time and money, and he urged them to be patient.

Rebuilding Afghanistan would be a long and expensive road. Karzai urged the public to "be patient."

The Reemergence of the Taliban

Karzai had barely taken office in 2004 when a violent insurgency in the south threatened to derail his plans. The Taliban were back. Karzai insisted that the insurgency had help from outsiders such as al Qaeda and Iran's Revolutionary Guard. He especially blamed Pakistan for giving the Taliban sanctuary and the Pakistani ISI for sending suicide bombers and Taliban foot soldiers into Afghanistan.

Karzai sounded the alarm in Washington, but U.S. forces were was busy in Iraq. He had a warm relationship with President Bush, but their contact had dwindled to not much more than a weekly telephone call. Meanwhile, foreign aid and security forces kept going where rebuilding was easiest: in Kabul and the more stable north and west. The huge southern provinces of Kandahar and Helmand had been, according to Herold, "left to rot,"[45] and that is where the Taliban were making the greatest inroads.

Karzai's Amnesty Offer

In 2005 Karzai tried negotiating with the Taliban. He offered Taliban militants (except for Mullah Omar and about a hundred other most-wanted fugitives) amnesty in exchange for renouncing violence. This gesture angered many Afghans who had suffered at the hands of the Taliban or Northern Alliance warlords. The Afghan people wanted known criminals arrested, prosecuted, and punished, not offered a respectable place in society.

Karzai argued that arrests and trials would only incite more violence. He defended the amnesty as the best hope for peace:

> If I can reduce the bomb blasts in Afghanistan by bringing some of the Taliban home, and put things in order by making them behave all right, then I should do that. Now, if you ask me as a citizen of Afghanistan, "Karzai, what is it that you want, justice or peace?," I would say, of course, both—most human beings would. But, if you ask me as the

The Insurgency

The coalition and Karzai's Afghan forces are busy fighting a number of different rebel groups generally called "the insurgency." What the guerrilla insurgents have in common is hatred of the West and desire for power. Their religious fanaticism varies.

The biggest and most extreme rebel group is the Taliban, Islamic fundamentalists who went underground after the 2001 coalition attack and who are making a very strong comeback. Other Afghan Islamic militants and warlords are fighting alongside the Taliban to drive out the non-Islamic Western forces. These include the Haqqani network and the Hezb-i-Islami network. Finally, foreign fighters—Arab terrorists, Pakistani militants—have joined the insurgency, partly to destroy the coalition (whom they see as invaders) and partly to destroy Karzai (whom they see as a tool of the invaders).

President of Afghanistan, then I have to say, "Peace gives you continuation of life. Justice does not, necessarily."[46]

Karzai's move had some success. Four senior Taliban officials and more than twenty low-level members laid down their arms and accepted the authority of the Karzai government.

Safe in the Green Zone

Beginning in 2006, small, unorganized Afghan- and NATO-led forces replaced American troops in the south. The new coalition forces went after the insurgents with heavy-handed strikes that were not always well coordinated. The unintended result was more destruction and many civilian casualties, which began to turn the Afghan people against the Western coalition. Meanwhile, Taliban attacks spread into the east and north, including Kabul.

As suicide bombings in Kabul increased, frightened residents demanded better security. Blocked-off areas were secured by 10-foot-high concrete blast walls (3m) and patched together into a heavily patrolled sector called the Green Zone. The international civilian community—diplomats, UN and embassy staff, aid agencies, foreign businesspeople—clustered in the zone. So did wealthy Afghans and Karzai government officials. The Green Zone became the safest place in the capital. It also became a bubble that kept people inside from understanding the growing unrest outside Kabul.

Karzai's Refugee Problem

Stopping the spread of the insurgency was complicated by Karzai's refugee problem. Between 2002 and 2008, the UN High Commission for Refugees helped some 5 million Afghans, mostly rural villagers, return to Afghanistan. An estimated 3 million more refugees were waiting or afraid to return, despite pressure from Pakistani and Iranian officials who told them it was safe to go home (so the refugee camps could be shut down).

The refugees who did come back dreamed of new jobs and

Many Afghan regugees had been gone for twenty years or more, and had no home when they returned. Refugee camps like Chami-Babrak quickly became overcrowded.

their old homelands. Many of them, however, had been away for twenty years or more. Their villages had been either destroyed by war or taken over long ago by others. All over Afghanistan, masses of poor returnees had nowhere to go. They drifted to the cities, where they set up tent camps on the outskirts that lacked even basic services. These soon became critically overcrowded.

A typical example was Chami-Babrak outside Kabul. There, two hundred displaced Afghan families lived under blankets propped up by bamboo poles. They had no water, electricity, or waste disposal. They got by as day laborers or by begging in downtown Kabul, where the unemployment rate topped 40 percent. Poor returnees could see brand-new high-rise hotels and office buildings from their tent camps on the edges of cities. They heard reports that Karzai had received $10 billion in foreign aid earmarked for refugee relief, but they saw none of that money. Angrily, they blamed corruption in the Karzai government for their troubles.

Karzai's Other Refugee Problem

Poor returnees were not the only Afghans who were dissatisfied with conditions in Afghanistan. The country had a serious brain drain, and there was little to entice professionals and other bright and ambitious Afghans to come back. According to Obaid Younossi, who returned after living in the United States for twenty-six years: "Afghans with an education and the skills in greatest demand know they can earn far more and live far better abroad. For example, university professors make less than $2 per hour in Afghanistan, and licensed physicians make about $100 a month working in a government hospital."[47]

Plenty of people who did come back were old enemies who brought their old resentments and agendas with them. Communists, mujahideen exiles, and ethnic minorities all wanted a stake in the new Afghanistan.

The mujahideen warlords who had stayed in Afghanistan to fight the Soviets and the Taliban were even more disgruntled. Many had left school when they were young to fight for their country and kept fighting as one conflict followed another. Now they were uneducated, hardened veterans without seats in the parliament or top posts in the government, police, or military. The jobs they felt entitled to were filled by educated returnees in the effort to make government more efficient. (These technocrat returnees get no respect from the warlords and their tribesmen. All over the country they are known as "dogwashers.")

The influx of returnees, rich or poor, caused Afghanistan's population to boom. The last official Afghan national census was conducted in 1979, the year of the Soviet invasion. That year the total population was 15.5 million. In 2003, a UN estimate put the total population at 23.9 million, 2.5 million in Kabul alone. During Karzai's first term in office—a span of only five years—the country's population rose to an estimated 28.2 million, and Kabul swelled by an additional 1 million people. All these people needed food, power, and health care. The sketchy electrical grid and the already struggling social service agencies buckled under the demand.

Public Revolt

Karzai was least able to provide services, improvements, or protection in rural areas. He barely had time to meet with delegations of tribal elders from rural provinces, who by 2005 were waiting months for an audience with Karzai. Some walked all the way to Kabul to plead for help. More and more were blaming Karzai personally when help did not arrive. According to Anderson, Karzai faced a chorus of respectful but pointed complaints from a group of Badakhshan tribal elders at a palace audience in 2005: "People are beginning to tell us that we shouldn't have voted for you, because you cannot defend us. … Lately, people have been coming up to me and saying, 'You [Karzai] haven't fulfilled your promises.' … I am thinking that the Afghan government has forgotten us."[48]

Polite pleas for help turned to rioting in Jalalabad in May 2005. Anderson explains:

Due to growing public unrest, President Karzai increased his personal security when he faced many angry tribal elders in 2005. Some had been waiting for months to speak with him.

On the first night of rioting, copies of an anonymous letter circulated in the streets of Kabul. This Night Letter, as it was called, was a vehement exhortation to Afghans to oppose Karzai, whom it accused of being un-Islamic, an ally of the Taliban, and a "U.S.A. servant." The letter said that Karzai had put the interests of his "evil master" ahead of those of Afghans, and it called for leaders who were proven patriots, mujahideen—[meaning] members of the Northern Alliance, many of whom are now warlords and regional strongmen— to defy him.[49]

Public unrest got worse in Kabul on May 29, 2006, the 8th of Jowza in the Afghan calendar. In what became known as the 8th of Jowza revolt, mobs shouted "Down with Karzai!" along with anti-American slogans and burned posters of Karzai. The rioters were mostly young men and students fed up with coalition bombings of civilians and foreign aid going to U.S. contractors and the pockets of Afghan businesspeople. The Afghan police could not restore order.

Moving Backward

Karzai found it difficult to address one problem without creating another. For example, he tried to mollify the warlords by bringing them into his government and allowing them seats in parliament. That provoked public anger, however, and charges that he was dealing with corrupt criminals whose past crimes should be punished.

Karzai tried to soothe public anger by promising to right past wrongs. He announced plans to create tribunals to try war criminals and vowed to crack down on corruption in his government. That, too, backfired. The warlords in his parliament, who would likely be the defendants at those tribunals, promptly passed an amnesty law that forgave all their past crimes. Some began making trouble for Karzai by stirring up old ethnic and tribal rivalries at public rallies. All of this chipped away at Karzai's authority.

Late in his first term, Karzai also came under fire for allowing

Convincing Farmers Not to Grow Poppy

The Karzai government, along with foreign agencies such as the U.S. Agency for International Development, set out to discourage poor farmers from growing poppy by giving them alternative, better-paying ways to make a living. In Helmand Province, this involved hiring local farmers for small public-works projects—building roads, for example, or cleaning out the silt from a huge network of old irrigation canals. Once the workers started getting paychecks, government teams moved in to cut down the poppy fields. The idea was to follow up that effort with long-term, multimillion-dollar infrastructure projects that would raise the standard of living for everyone.

At first, the cash-for-work project in Helmand seemed to be working. Then the trouble started. Powerful landowners bribed the police not to cut down their poppy fields, and provincial officials kept the opium smuggling routes open. Worst of all, workers were intimidated, ambushed, and murdered, either by Taliban or by poppy growers who did not want anything to threaten their profitable business. Karzai could not secure the countryside, so local people obeyed the Taliban to make the violence stop. As relief worker Joel Hafvenstein writes, "Security was the real currency of Afghanistan. The traumatized population of Helmand would trade anything for it, follow anyone who could offer it."

Quoted in William Grimes, "Afghan Struggle to Change Poppy Fields into Roads," *New York Times*, November 7, 2007. www.nytimes.com/2007/11/07/books/07grim.html.

The opium poppy is used to make heroin.

the passage of the Shiite Personal Status Law. This controversial law required women in Afghanistan's Shiite Muslim minority to obey their husbands in line with sharia. (The original wording required "readiness for sex and not leaving the house without the husband's permission."[50]) Karzai had promised to amend the law, but did not. Women's rights advocates accused him of pushing it through in exchange for votes from Shiite clerics, which further hurt his image.

Mocked as "the Mayor of Kabul"

The result of the public protests and Karzai's weak efforts was twofold. Many Afghans began to view him as a U.S. puppet and an enemy of the people. Many others simply ignored him. Karzai was increasingly viewed as a man with no authority outside the Green Zone. All over the country, he was mocked as "the mayor of Kabul."

Karzai had wanted to come across as a unifier who was not controlled by any political party. He was now seen, however, as a weak leader without a party or movement that could defend him politically. Instead of the loyal tribal militias that physically protect Afghan leaders and give them all-important bargaining power, he was protected by an American security team. His own deputy president and defense minister, the Tajik commander Fahim, backed someone else in the 2004 presidential election. (Karzai kicked Fahim out of the government for his disloyalty.) Karzai had no better control over his cabinet ministers, a mix of mujahideen politicians and educated Afghan returnees who clashed constantly.

Put on the defensive, Karzai became a more savvy politician and a more suspicious, isolated man. He developed a shrewd style of making deals with one faction or another to get them to work together or support him. At the same time, he felt physically vulnerable and suspected coups on all sides. His sense of abandonment grew as Swiss and Dutch troops went home and U.S., British, Canadian, and Polish troop withdrawals were announced, beginning in 2011.

Targeted for Assassination

Karzai had good reason to think people were plotting against him. He has survived at least four assassination attempts since becoming interim president in 2002.

In September 2002, a gunman opened fire on Karzai in Kandahar City. Karzai was unhurt, but a bodyguard was killed. In September 2004, a Taliban rocket just missed his helicopter on his way to open a school in Gardez. In 2007 a barrage of rockets was aimed at Karzai as he delivered a speech in the city of Ghazni. Karzai calmly finished his speech before being whisked to safety.

The worst attack occurred in April 2008 in Kabul while Karzai was viewing an Independence Day military parade. A hit squad launched rocket-propelled grenades and fired automatic weapons at the viewing stand, killing three people and wounding ten others. Again, Karzai was not hurt. The Taliban claimed

President Karzai at an Independence Day parade. Automatic gunfire broke out at the ceremony, forcing dignitaries, including the president, to take cover.

responsibility. When a Taliban spokesman was asked if the hit men intended to kill Karzai, he replied, "Our aim was not to directly hit someone. We just wanted to show the world that we can attack anywhere we want to."[51]

Cause for Optimism

Karzai was running out of time and options to stop the insurgency. There was cause for optimism, however, when a new administration came to power in Washington, D.C., in 2008. The new U.S. president, Barack Obama, had made commitment to the war in Afghanistan a major campaign issue. Karzai hoped that a new U.S. leader would make it possible for him to assert his own leadership.

Chapter 5

Karzai's Uncertain Future

Torn between conflicting demands, Karzai seems to be losing his grip on Afghanistan, and the West seems to be losing its grip on Karzai. For the time being, however, no one else appears to be a better candidate for the job. The permanent institutions that can maintain national stability and security during a change in leadership, such as trustworthy law enforcement and justice systems, are not yet strong in Afghanistan. Whether the Karzai government proves to be another Afghan regime whose rise and fall depends on the strength or weakness of its leader remains to be seen.

U.S. Policy Under Obama

President Obama made good on his pledge to devote more resources to the war in Afghanistan. Between February 2009 and May 2010, the number of U.S. troops deployed as part of the NATO-led mission in Afghanistan increased from 38,000 to 94,000. This marked the first time since 2003 that more U.S. troops were in Afghanistan than were serving in Iraq. The main job of these additional troops is to train and equip the ANA, which reached a goal of 134,000 trained soldiers in August 2010. The Afghan army's ability to operate independently of NATO forces, however, is uncertain.

As the insurgency worsened, coalition casualties increased. As of September 2010, 2,069 coalition troops had been killed

President Obama increased U.S. troops deployed in Afghanistan by 40 percent to help train and equip Afghan security forces.

in Afghanistan; 1,271 were U.S. soldiers. With so much work still to do in Afghanistan, the possibility of withdrawing U.S. forces beginning in July 2011, as scheduled, is remote. A 2010 Congressional Research Service report calculates the United States has so far spent $308 billion in Afghanistan, divided among military operations, foreign aid, Afghan reconstruction, and training of Afghan security forces.

The 2009 Presidential Election

Karzai's first term in office was up in 2009. He ran for reelection in a chaotic field of forty-three candidates. Typical of Karzai's deal-making style, Fahim was back in the picture as Karzai's running mate. Despite their earlier falling-out, Karzai had brought the Tajik military commander back into the government as an advisor and "marshal for life" in 2006, when the insurgency heated up. In 2009, putting Fahim on the ticket for vice president was calculated to bring Karzai more Tajik votes.

In 2004 international backing had made Karzai the front-runner for the presidency. In 2009, however, Karzai was a seasoned politician; shrewd Afghan alliances such as the Fahim partnership made him the front-runner. His closest rival was Abdullah Abdullah, the Tajik doctor who was Karzai's foreign minister in 2002.

The election took place on August 20, 2009. The results were delayed, however, because of charges of fraud leveled at Karzai and other candidates. For weeks votes were recounted, and a fraud investigation was launched. In the meantime, Karzai claimed victory. This proved embarrassing when a special Electoral Complaints Commission concluded that there had been massive vote rigging: A third of Karzai's total, more than 1 million votes, turned out to be fake.

UN and U.S. officials pressured Karzai to hold a runoff election with Abdullah, scheduled for November 7. On November 1, however, Abdullah withdrew in protest, saying an honest, transparent election was impossible. The next day, Karzai was declared president for a second five-year term.

Election controversies had weakened public trust in Karzai, however. Fahim (now with the title of first vice president) had been accused of criminal activities such as kidnapping for ransom, and it did not look good to many voters to see the old warlord on the ticket. Neither did it look good when, after the election, Karzai gave himself the right to appoint all five Electoral Complaints Commission members and stripped the commission of its powers.

Achievements and Failures

Karzai worked to repair his image by focusing on reconstruction successes. In a January 2010 interview with ABC's Diane Sawyer, for example, Karzai touted his government's achievements:

> The Afghan government is providing services. We provide

Abdullah Abdullah, one of President Karzai's challengers in the 2009 election, has said that Karzai's government would not be able to rein in corruption and has wasted the resources and lives of its international allies.

electricity. We provide water. We provide health services. We provide education. We have a thriving marketplace in Afghanistan.

When we came to power in 2002, Afghanistan's per capita [per person average] income was a mere $150. Today, it's nearly $500. We had almost no schools, no universities.

Today, we have nearly 7 million children going to school. We [had] from two or three universities that hardly functioned, we are nearly 15 universities, plus private universities in numerous numbers ... and over 40,000 students. ... Our health service is a *lot*—a lot more better.[52]

There is no question, however, that the pace of progress has been painfully slow. High unemployment and grinding poverty has also fueled the ongoing insurgency, because the Taliban is attracting recruits by paying them. As one Pakistani journalist writes, "A good portion of the fighters for the Taliban are, in fact, day laborers. The term 'the $10 Taliban' has been coined of late. ... They aren't necessarily connected to [Taliban beliefs], but in order to survive and make a living ... they do join the fight."[53]

There is also no question that Karzai's authority is limited. According to Lamb:

Karzai's biggest challenge is ... the fact that almost nobody in Afghanistan takes any notice of him. ... Karzai passes laws ensuring press freedom, and ministers send police or army officers to deliver death threats or arrest journalists who criticize them. He lifted the Taliban's ban on music and satellite television, only for his own judges to reintroduce it. Warlords such as Ismael Khan in the west collect border taxes and customs duties and refuse to pass them on. Even Karzai's wife ignores his wishes. "When I go home she doesn't let me choose the television channel," he laughs.[54]

Corruption in the Government and the Family

Corruption—using a position of trust to profit dishonestly—is also slowing the pace of reconstruction. Campaign corruption is just one kind of corruption in the Afghan government. There is petty corruption: low-level employees who have to be bribed to get things done. There is large-scale corruption by ministers, top

Ahmed Wali Karzai, brother of Afghan President Hamid Karzai, speaking during a meeting with elders in Kandahar province. Three of Karzai's brothers have been accused of corruption within the Afghan government.

officials, and their relatives, who get kickbacks from international contracts or a cut of drug profits. There are legal loopholes that allow foreign contractors to receive government funds to do a job, subcontract the job to Afghans for less, and pocket the rest.

Three of Karzai's brothers have been accused of one or more of these forms of corruption. Qayum, Mahmoud, and Ahmed Wali all came back to Afghanistan when Hamid rose to power. All three have extensive political or business interests there, and all are powerful figures behind the president.

Karzai's speeches contain strong words about rooting out corruption, but in practice he tends to ignore the problem or issue conflicting denials and excuses. When confronted with his brothers' questionable activities, for example, he shrugs and says he cannot control what they do. When pressed by U.S. vice president Joseph Biden in 2009, Karzai insisted that there was no corruption at all in his government, and besides, it was not his fault.

The Brothers Karzai

Allegations of corruption in the Karzai government hit close to home. Three Karzai brothers have become rich, powerful, and controversial since 2001. Qayum held a seat in parliament from 2001 to 2008, then resigned after other members charged that he was never there. He is involved in behind-the-scenes negotiations, sometimes with the Taliban.

Mahmoud has built a business empire, some say by demanding and getting sweetheart deals, which are contracts that give him special terms and unfair advantages, from U.S. investors and government officials. He is a partner in the country's only cement factory and on the board of directors of the Kabul Bank. He is part owner of the country's Toyota dealerships and four coal mines. With millions in loans from the U.S. government Overseas Private Investment Corporation, he built a sprawling housing community in Kandahar on 10,000 acres (4,047ha) given to him by Kandahar officials.

Ahmed Wali, one of those officials, has built a political empire. He is head of the provincial council of Kandahar, a power broker known as the "king of Kandahar." He is said to take a cut of most business transactions in Kandahar, including narcotics trafficking. Corruption charges include money laundering, influence peddling, and ballot-box stuffing in 2009. He is also on the U.S. payroll; the Central Intelligence Agency pays him to recruit Afghans for CIA counterinsurgency operations in Kandahar.

A view from the Palm Jumeirah in Dubai, United Arab Emirates. Mahmoud Karzai says he made at least $800,000 by buying and then reselling a high-end Dubai villa using a loan provided by the chairman of the troubled Kabul Bank, and that he bought the house on the Palm Jumeirah in July 2007 to obtain residency in Dubai.

Bashing the West

Since the U.S. war in Afghanistan began in 2001, U.S. military and financial aid to Afghanistan, as well as the U.S. death toll, has far exceeded that of any other foreign country. Nevertheless, a growing theme of Karzai's public comments is criticism of the United States and the U.S.-UK presence in Afghanistan. Some is subtle. For example, Karzai told ABC's Sawyer in January 2010 that he was grateful to the United States for "the little help" and "the little money"[55] Afghanistan has received. In June 2010, amid a flurry of excited news about the discovery of $1 trillion in untapped mineral deposits in Afghanistan, a potential godsend for the Afghan economy, Karzai announced that it was only fair that mining rights should go to countries that had helped Afghanistan massively in recent years. The first priority, he said, should go to Japan.

Some of Karzai's criticism of the West is not so subtle. Asked in March 2009 if he welcomed the U.S. troop surge, Karzai said, "They're seven years too late."[56] Later in 2009, he accused the British and Americans of wanting the Taliban to take over the south so Western countries could keep their troops in Afghanistan.

Increasingly, Karzai has reacted to criticism by losing his temper. His wildest anti-American, anti-Western tirades came in early April 2010. In a speech in Kabul, he accused the UN and the West of committing the fraud in the 2009 presidential election. He described the coalition as being akin to invaders, which, he said, would make the insurgency a legitimate resistance movement. Then he fired off a threat to his supporters in parliament: "If you and the international community pressure me more, I swear that I am going to join the Taliban."[57]

The West Bashes Back

Americans promptly fired back at Karzai. Former UN envoy to Afghanistan Peter Galbraith described Karzai as "slightly off-balance" and suggested he was a drug user: "He's prone to tirades. He can be very emotional, act impulsively. In fact, some of the

Secretary of State Hillary Clinton, left, and Afghan President Hamid Karzai shake hands at a news conference in the State Department. Secretary Clinton has expressed her lack of faith in Afghanistan's ability to rid corruption in the government.

palace insiders say that he has a certain fondness for some of Afghanistan's most profitable exports."[58]

Secretary of State Hillary Clinton, who had called Afghanistan a "narco-state" that was "plagued by limited capacity and widespread corruption"[59] a year earlier, suggested that the White House might cancel Karzai's planned visit to Washington in May. Tempers cooled, however, and Karzai made the scheduled trip to Washington for meetings with Obama and Clinton. The fraying relationship appeared to have been patched up during the visit, if joint remarks about being reliable partners and handshakes and smiles for press photographers were to be believed.

Tensions rose again in June 2010, however, with unconfirmed reports that Karzai was secretly meeting with rebel leader Sirajuddin Haqqani, presumably to cut his own deal with the insurgents. Political analysts speculate that, with the U.S.-NATO counterinsurgency floundering, Karzai is preparing for U.S. withdrawal by negotiating with Haqqani and his backers in Pakistan.

How to Survive Politically

Karzai knows that many Afghans resent the presence of foreign forces. Karzai also remembers the Taliban's gruesome murder of Najibullah after the Soviets withdrew from his country, and he does not want to suffer the same fate if the Taliban take over after Western troops withdraw. *Time* magazine editor Tony Karon suggests, therefore, that Karzai snipes at the Western military presence because that is what he has to do to survive politically: "While he may have been installed by a U.S.-led invasion, if Karzai is to survive the departure of Western forces, he will have to reinvent himself as a national leader with an independent power base. So from Karzai's point of view, he's pushing back against the U.S. ... because he *must*."[60]

In contrast, Max Boot of the Council on Foreign Relations says Karzai should be spending less time criticizing Western forces and more time acting like a wartime leader if he wants to survive: "Rarely if ever does he visit his own troops in the field, go to hospitals to comfort the wounded or honor the dead. ... Karzai doesn't even give speeches to rally his people in the effort to defeat the Taliban."[61]

The Risks of Biting the Hand That Feeds Him

Admirers and critics alike say Karzai is taking a big risk by biting the hand that feeds him, and the Taliban knows it. Karzai, after all, depends on American assistance and support. As Taliban mullah Abdul Salam Zaeef told war reporter Scott Taylor: "The government has no control; they have no power. ... [Karzai] is crying in front of the media. He is powerless. If the U.S. military were to withdraw, the Karzai government would not last a week."[62]

Taliban spokesmen also say the ANA is powerless to stop the insurgency on its own. They could be right; as one rank-and-file Afghan soldier told Taylor, "The Taliban is number one. That's why they are always kicking our [butts]."[63]

As for Afghans who work for Western military or aid organizations, most know that Karzai is unable to protect them, with or without coalition help. An Afghan security guard accompanying Taylor to a Taliban stronghold in Kandahar told him fatalistically, "You are lucky, sir, because you are a foreigner. ... If the Taliban captures us, they will either kill you right away or hold you for ransom. For Afghans caught working for the infidels, it will mean torture before they finally kill us. ... Promise me that if we are taken, you will kill me before they torture me."[64]

The Risks of *Not* Biting the Hand That Feeds Him

The Taliban-led insurgency is not Karzai's only enemy. If Karzai does *not* take a stand against the West, he could be facing a new Northern Alliance of disgruntled, anti-Western Tajiks and Uzbeks who supported Abdullah in the 2009 election. At a tribal gathering in Northern Alliance territory, where even in 2004 the vote for Karzai was just 1 percent, an Afghan *maskhara,* or entertainer, named Samad Pashean made this prediction: "We Afghans have to learn how to eat for ourselves, like cows, who, with their cuds, know how to find the good stuff to eat, and how to spit out the bad. ... One day, we Afghans will be able to spit out Karzai."[65]

Karzai had hoped that giving the warlords seats in parliament would persuade them to support a strong central government. That has not worked. The warlords balked at disarming their private militias or merging them with the Afghan army. They used their positions in Kabul not to help the country but to give themselves even more power in the regions they control. Many Afghans want U.S. forces to stay in Afghanistan, but the warlords want Karzai to protect their interests, not the interests of what they view as a foreign military occupation.

Physical and Emotional Exhaustion

Karzai walks a fine line, and there are signs that he is tiring of the balancing act. Rubin noted physical signs that the pressure was

Afghan President Hamid Karzai has shown signs of strain during his presidency, including a short temper and a nervous tic.

getting to him in the summer of 2009: "He's skin and bones. He always has a cold or a cough and takes effervescent vitamin-C tablets compulsively. ... 'He is stressed, short of patience, short of temper,' a friend said. He snaps easily. Promotes flatterers. Kills the messenger. And his twitching eye—a nervous tic, they say—is unusually active."[66]

Karzai describes himself as worn out: "I'm a very, very, very simple person. I have no property. I have no money. I have no love for luxury. ... I'm an exhausted person. I've not begun this seven years ago. I've begun this when I was 22. I've not had a private life since then. I deserve one. I long for one. ... The moment I get this choice, I would leave."[67]

Of course, no one is forcing Karzai to stay in office. His suggestions that he would leave if only he could may be an example of his theatrical nature. Karzai is not being coy about his few assets, however. In June 2010, an Afghan anticorruption commission report revealed that he earns $525 a month as president, owns no land or property, and has less than $20,000 in the bank. (The commission did not count assets owned by the other Karzai brothers.)

Longtime friend Christina Lamb described the erratic Karzai as a paranoid shut-in when she visited the president in August 2009: "I had to pass through seven layers of security. … Karzai is flanked by 10 gunmen and monitored by snipers just to walk the 100 yards between his office and home. A keen walker, his

Cocooned in the Palace

As security around the president tightens, Karzai complains about his inability to move freely. Aside from his daily brisk walk around the grounds of the Arg, he spends more and more time indoors. Reporters said he spent a visit to Britain's Prince Charles's house in Scotland walking the moors for hours like a man let out of prison.

Outwardly confident, Karzai is still a gracious host to visitors at the Arg. He likes to serve them his favorite Afghan almonds and grapes and strong Afghan coffee. According to journalist Jason Burke:

> Impressive in Western capitals, Karzai is at his best in Kabul. …"He's well-read, funny and can talk about everything from 19th-century politics to poetry to pots," says one Westerner who has dealt closely with him. Karzai is also charismatic and, for a head of state, unpretentious. His abrupt, exuberant hand gestures give the impression of energy and decision. In interviews, he often sits on the edge of his chair, listening intently, apparently barely able to contain his desire to act.

Jason Burke, "Hard Man in a Hard Country," *Guardian/Observer*, July 20, 2008. www. guardian.co.uk/world/2008/jul/20/afghanistan.

exercise is now confined to pacing around his small walled garden with its two baby deer."[68] She reports that all of his food is first sampled by a team of personal tasters, just in case it is poisoned.

A Damaged Peace Jirga and Demoralizing Leaks

Against all odds, the idealistic Karzai keeps trying to bring peace to Afghanistan. On June 2–4, 2010, he held a so-called Peace Jirga designed to reach out to the Taliban (or as Fahim put it, "to find a peaceful life for those Afghans who are unhappy"[69]) and call a truce. Washington was pretty unhappy that Karzai was willing to deal with the people who were shooting at American soldiers, but Karzai would not back down.

Afghan President Hamid Karzai, center, listen to speeches delivered by delegates during a three day conference of Peace Jirga in Kabul, Afghanistan.

The council drew a half-million people to Mazar-i-Sharif, the site of several key battles and tragic massacres since 1978. Unfortunately, there was no laying down of arms at the Peace Jirga. The Taliban not only refused to attend (or negotiate at all until all foreign forces leave the country) but also launched rockets into the meeting during Karzai's opening speech and sent more than a dozen suicide bombers into the city. Karzai endorsed the jirga's goodwill gestures anyway. He asked that Taliban members' names be removed from the international terrorist blacklist and that all Taliban suspects in Afghan jails and U.S. custody be released if there was not enough evidence to hold them there. Many saw this as another sign that Karzai is distancing himself from the West and aligning himself with America's enemy.

Karzai's goodwill gestures did not seem to have any effect on Taliban offensives or brutality. In July 2010, a cache of some ninety-two thousand military reports known as the Afghan War Diary was leaked on the website Wikileaks. Analysts concluded from the reports that the Taliban is stronger now than at any time since 2001. Afghan warlords such as Gulbuddin Hekmatyar, who tends to switch sides depending on who is winning, have formed alliances with the Taliban. Mullah Omar, hiding in Pakistan amid a swirl of rumors that he is either under arrest or being protected by the ISI, issued a June 2010 directive ordering Taliban forces to kill Afghan civilians, including women, as well as coalition forces and anyone working for coalition forces. This was a dramatic about-face from previous orders to avoid harming civilians.

Down but Not Out

Hamid Karzai is undeniably a patriot. Nine years of frustration and failure to bring peace to Afghanistan have undoubtedly worn him down. Although his future as Afghan president and place in Afghan history are uncertain, his belief in his ability to forge coalitions between past enemies, for the good of Afghanistan, is unshaken.

So is Karzai's hope of achieving his goals through nonviolence and with honor, guiding principles in more than thirty years of wartime resistance: "We must be seeking peace and peaceful means. ... We must be conducting this war as better human beings because we are better than the guys that are fighting us. We must *prove* that we are better than the guys that are fighting us."[70] For both Karzai and Afghanistan, whether this is ultimately possible remains to be seen.

Introduction: The Afghan Partner in America's Longest War

1. George W. Bush, "The President's Address to the Nation on the Use of Force in Afghanistan, October 7, 2001," C-SPAN. www.c-span.org/executive/bush_war.asp?Cat=Current_Event&Code=Bush_Admin.

2. Quoted in Thomas Nagorski, "Editor's Notebook: Afghan War Now Country's Longest," ABC News, June 7, 2010. http://abcnews.go.com/Politics/afghan-war-now-longest-war-us-history/story?id=10849303.

3. Osama bin Laden, "Osama bin Laden, Videotaped Address, October 7, 2001," University of Chicago Press. www.press.uchicago.edu/Misc/Chicago/481921texts.html.

4. Nagorski, "Editor's Notebook."

5. Haseeb Humayoon, *Afghanistan Report 4: The Reelection of Hamid Karzai.* Washington, DC: Institute for the Study of War, 2010, p. 6.

6. Ishtiaq Ahmad, "Combating Terrorism Beyond Bush, Karzai and Musharraf," Weekly Pulse, May 16–22, 2008. www.ishtiaqahmad.com/item_display.aspx?listing_id=152&listing_type=1.

7. Quoted in Nick B. Mills, *Karzai: The Failing American Intervention and the Struggle for Afghanistan.* New York: Wiley, 2007, p. 182.

Chapter 1: The Dutiful Son

8. Quoted in Mills, *Karzai,* p. 26.

9. Quoted in Mills, *Karzai,* p. 26.

10. Mills, *Karzai,* p. 32.

11. Quoted in Mills, *Karzai,* p. 32.

12. Quoted in Mills, *Karzai,* p. 37.

13. Quoted in Mills, *Karzai,* p. 33.

14. Quoted in Academy of Achievement, "Hamid Karzai

Interview," June 2, 2002. Revised October 9, 2006. www. achievement.org/autodoc/page/kar0int-1.

15. Quoted in Academy of Achievement, "Hamid Karzai Interview."

16. Quoted in Mills, *Karzai*, p. 29.

17. Quoted in Mills, *Karzai*, p. 39.

18. Quoted in Academy of Achievement, "Hamid Karzai Interview."

19. Quoted in Academy of Achievement, "Hamid Karzai Interview."

20. Elizabeth Rubin, "Karzai in His Labyrinth," New York Times Sunday Magazine, August 9, 2009. www.nytimes .com/2009/08/09/magazine/09Karzai-t.html.

21. Quoted in Francis X. Clines, "A Nation Challenged: The Family; For Afghan Leader, Support of Another Sort," New York Times, December 17, 2001. www.nytimes.com/2001/12/17/ us/nation-challenged-family-for-afghan-leader-american-support-another-sort.html?pagewanted=all.

22. Quoted in Clines, "A Nation Challenged."

23. Quoted in Jon Lee Anderson, "The Man in the Palace," New Yorker, June 6, 2005. www.newyorker.com /archive/2005/06/06/050606fa_fact_anderson.

Chapter 2: Driving Out a Superpower

24. Quoted in Academy of Achievement, "Hamid Karzai Interview."

25. Quoted in Robert D. Kaplan, *Soldiers of God: With Islamic Warriors in Afghanistan and Pakistan*. New York: Vintage, 2001, p. 196.

26. Quoted in Nick B. Mills, "My Nights with Hamid," Foreign Policy, November 19, 2009. www.foreignpolicy.com /articles/2009/11/19/my_nights_with_hamid.

27. Quoted in Mills, *Karzai*, p. 73.

28. Rubin, "Karzai in His Labyrinth."

29. Quoted in Academy of Achievement, "Hamid Karzai Interview."

30. Quoted in Academy of Achievement, "Hamid Karzai Interview."

31. Christina Lamb, "President of Hell: Hamid Karzai's Battle to Govern Post-war, Post-Taliban Afghanistan," Sunday Times (London), June 29, 2003. www.timesonline.co.uk/tol/life_and_style/article1143612.ece.

32. Quoted in Lamb, "President of Hell."

Chapter 3: Driving Out the Taliban

33. Sunday Times (London), "Looking a Little Like the King of Kabul," Fox News U.S. & World feed, January 23, 2003. www.foxnews.com/story/0,2933,44641,00.html.

34. Quoted in Mills, *Karzai*, p. 148.

35. Quoted in Mills, *Karzai*, p. 159.

36. Quoted in Mills, *Karzai*, pp. 159–60.

37. Rubin, "Karzai in His Labyrinth."

38. Quoted in Rubin, "Karzai in His Labyrinth."

39. Jon Lee Anderson, "After the Revolution," New Yorker, January 28, 2002. www.newyorker.com/archive/2002/01/28/020128fa_FACT1.

40. Quoted in Asian Political News, "Gucci Designer Picks Afghan Leader Karzai as Most Fashionable," January 21, 2002. http://findarticles.com/p/articles/mi_m0WDQ/is_2002_Jan_21/ai_83916816.

41. Anderson, "The Man in the Palace."

42. Quoted in Christina Lamb, "Hamid Karzai: The Friendly Anglophile Who Alienated the West," Sunday Times (London), November 22, 2009. www.timesonline.co.uk/tol/news/world/afghanistan/article6927087.ece.

Chapter 4: President Karzai

43. William Grimes, "Afghan Struggle to Change Poppy Fields into Roads," New York Times, November 7, 2007. www.nytimes.com/2007/11/07/books/07grim.html.

44. Marc W. Herold, "Hat Trick: Selling Brand Karzai," Cursor, March 10, 2006. http://cursor.org/stories/emptyspace3.html.

45. Herold, "Hat Trick."

46. Quoted in Anderson, "The Man in the Palace."

47. Obaid Younossi, "A Brain Drain Threatens Afghanistan's Future," New York Times, February 9, 2006. www.nytimes.com/2006/02/09/opinion/09iht-edyounossi.html.
48. Quoted in Anderson, "The Man in the Palace."
49. Anderson, "The Man in the Palace."
50. Quoted in Jim Sciutto, Bruno Roeber, and Nick Schifrin, "Afghanistan President Hamid Karzai Passes Controversial Law Limiting Women's Rights," ABC News, August 14, 2009. http://abcnews.go.com/International/story?id=8327666.
51. Quoted in AFP News Agency, "Afghan President Escapes Deadly Parade Attack," Haaba, April 27, 2008. www.haaba.com/news/2008/04/26/7-125764/afghan-president-escapes-deadly-parade-attack-two-killed.htm.

Chapter 5: Karzai's Uncertain Future

52. Quoted in ABC News, "ABC's Diane Sawyer Interviews Afghan President Hamid Karzai," transcript, January 12, 2010. http://abcnews.go.com/WN/Afghanistan/abcs-diane-sawyer-interviews-afghan-president-hamid-karzai/story?id=9544477.
53. Quoted in J.J. Green, "The Taliban Preempting the Surge," WTOP, January 22, 2010. www.wtop.com/?nid=778&sid=1870314.
54. Lamb, "President of Hell."
55. Quoted in ABC News, "ABC's Diane Sawyer Interviews Afghan President Hamid Karzai."
56. Quoted in Jim Lehrer, "Karzai: Additional U.S. Troops 'Seven Years Too Late,'" interview, PBS NewsHour, March 19, 2009. www.pbs.org/newshour/bb/asia/jan-june09/karzai_03-19.html.
57. Quoted in Alissa J. Rubin, "Karzai's Words Leave Few Choices for the West," New York Times, April 4, 2010. www.nytimes.com/2010/04/05/world/asia/05karzai.html.
58. Quoted in Daily Rundown, "U.S.-Afghan Rift Grows," MSNBC, April 6, 2010. http://afpakwar.com/blog/archives/4774.
59. Quoted in Ian Pannell, "Nosedive in Afghan-US Relations," BBC News, February 5, 2009. http://news.bbc.co.uk/2/hi/south_asia/7870340.stm.

60. Tony Karon, "Why Karzai Is Pushing Back Against the U.S.," Time, April 5, 2010. www.time.com/world/article/0,8599,1977781,00.html.
61. Max Boot, "The U.S. Needs to Teach Karzai a Thing or Two," Op-Ed, Council on Foreign Relations, November 1, 2009. www.cfr.org/publication/20707/us_needs_to_teach_hamid_karzai_a_thing_or_two.html.
62. Quoted in Scott Taylor, *Unembedded: Two Decades of Maverick War Reporting*. Vancouver, BC: Douglas & McIntyre, 2009, p. 346.
63. Quoted in Taylor, *Unembedded*, p. 319.
64. Quoted in Taylor, *Unembedded*, p. 328.
65. Quoted in Anderson, "The Man in the Palace."
66. Rubin, "Karzai in His Labyrinth."
67. Quoted in Rubin, "Karzai in His Labyrinth."
68. Christina Lamb, "Karzai's Paranoid World," Daily Beast, November 18, 2009. www.thedailybeast.com/blogs-and-stories/2009-11-18/the-karzai-i-know.
69. Quoted in Morning Star Online, "Afghanistan Opens Door to Militants," March 21, 2010. www.morningstaronline.co.uk/index.php/news/content/view/full/88232.
70. Hamid Karzai, "Governance, Growth and Development in Afghanistan," speech delivered at the Brookings Institution, Washington, DC, May 5, 2009. www.brooking.edu/~/media/Files/events/2009/0505_afghanistan/20090505_karzai.pdf, p. 15.

1957

Hamid Karzai is born December 24 in Karz, Kandahar Province, Afghanistan; his father is prominent Pashtun tribal leader Abdul Ahad Karzai.

1965

The Karzai family moves to the capital, Kabul, when Abdul Ahad Karzai is elected to the Afghan parliament.

1973

Muhammad Daoud, a royal cousin of Afghan king Zahir Shah, seizes power; Daoud abolishes the monarchy and proclaims Afghanistan a republic with himself as president.

1976

Karzai graduates from Habibia High School in Kabul and enters Himachal Pradesh University in Shimla, India.

1978

Communist coup topples the Daoud government. Karzai's father and uncle are imprisoned.

1979

The Soviet Union invades Afghanistan to support the Afghan Communist regime. A guerrilla insurgency of anti-Soviet mujahideen, backed by the United States, begins. Karzai's father and uncle are released from prison and go into exile in Pakistan.

1982

Karzai completes a master's degree in international relations and political science in India; joins his father and the Afghan resistance movement in exile in Quetta, Pakistan.

1989

Soviet forces withdraw from Afghanistan. The mujahideen continue to battle the Afghan Communist regime as well as each other.

1992

Kabul falls to mujahideen forces. Karzai returns to Afghanistan and is appointed deputy foreign minister in the coalition government of Burhanuddin Rabbani. The civil war between mujahideen factions, and the destruction of cities, intensifies.

1994–1995

Karzai returns to exile in Pakistan and works for the Taliban as chief fund-raiser.

1996

The Taliban takes over Afghanistan. Karzai, disillusioned by the regime's hard-line extremism and the growing influence of foreign terrorist groups such as al Qaeda, becomes a staunch opponent of the Taliban.

1999

Abdul Ahad Karzai is assassinated on July 14 in Pakistan. Karzai is named khan of the Popolzai clan; marries Zeenat Quraishi.

2001

Following the September 11 terrorist attacks, a U.S.-led coalition invades Afghanistan and topples the Taliban regime. The Bonn Conference selects Karzai to lead a six-month interim administration.

2002

A Loya Jirga selects Karzai as president of a two-year transitional government. Karzai survives an assassination attempt on September 5 in Kandahar.

2004

Karzai survives an assassination attempt on September 16 in Gardez. In November he wins Afghanistan's first democratic presidential election; takes office as His Excellency Hamid Karzai, President of the Islamic Republic of Afghanistan, on December 7.

2007

Karzai and Quraishi's son, Mirwais, is born on January 25 in Kabul. Karzai survives an assassination attempt on June 10 in Ghazni.

2008

Karzai survives an assassination attempt on April 18 in Kabul.

2009

U.S. and NATO forces continue to battle the strengthening Taliban insurgency. U.S. president Barack Obama orders an additional thirty thousand U.S. troops to Afghanistan. Karzai wins a second five-year term as president amid charges of election fraud and government corruption.

2010

U.S. troop levels in Afghanistan near 100,000. As of September, 2,069 coalition soldiers had been killed in Afghanistan; 1,271 were Americans.

For More Information

Books

Sarah Chayes, *The Punishment of Virtue: Inside Afghanistan After the Taliban.* New York: Penguin, 2007. A former National Public Radio reporter untangles the reasons for the ongoing violence in Afghanistan through her investigation of the murder of one of the good guys, the police chief of Kabul.

Lauri S. Friedman, ed., *Afghanistan: Introducing Issues with Opposing Viewpoints.* Farmington Hills, MI: Greenhaven, 2010. A useful anthology of expert opinion on current issues in Afghan politics and culture, placed in a pro/con format.

Joel Hafvenstein, *Opium Season: A Year on the Afghan Frontier.* Guilford, CT: Lyons, 2007. An American aid worker's account of helping thousands of Afghan opium poppy farmers make a legal living.

Malalai Joya, *A Woman Among Warlords.* New York: Scribner, 2009. Joya was elected to the Afghan parliament in 2005 at age twenty-seven, then suspended from parliament in 2007 for publicly denouncing fellow officials in the Karzai government as drug lords and criminals. She was named by *Time* magazine in 2010 as one of the one hundred most influential people in the world. Her outspoken autobiography offers unique insights into Afghanistan during Karzai's presidency.

Waseem Mahmood, *Good Morning Afghanistan.* Foreword by Hamid Karzai. London: Eye Books, 2007. A vivid account of post-Taliban Kabul and the radio program that became a lifeline of news and uncensored information for the Afghan people.

Periodicals

Peter W. Galbraith, "Why Hamid Karzai Makes a Bad Partner for the U.S.," *Washington Post,* April 8, 2010.

Selig S. Harrison, "A Smart Pashtun Play: Why Washington Should Back Karzai," *Newsweek,* July 6, 2010.

Michael Hastings, "The Runaway General," *Rolling Stone,* June 22, 2010.

Jason Motlagh, "With U.S. Approval, Moscow Heads Back to Afghanistan," *Time,* August 24, 2010.

Romesh Ratnesar and Aryn Baker, "An Inside Look at Hamid Karzai's Rising Woes," *Time,* September 10, 2006.

Daniel Schulman, "Karzai Said What?" *Mother Jones,* November 30, 2009.

Internet Sources

ABC News, "ABC's Diane Sawyer Interviews Afghan President Hamid Karzai," transcript, January 12, 2010. http://abcnews.go.com/WN/Afghanistan/abcs-diane-sawyer-interviews-afghan-president-hamid-karzai/story?id=9544477.

Max Boot, "Afghanistan: The Case for Optimism," Council on Foreign Relations, September 2, 2010. www.cfr.org/publication/22878/afghanistan.html.

Joel Brinkley, "The Hamid Karzai Problem," *San Francisco Chronicle,* August 15, 2010. http://articles.sfgate.com/2010-08-15/opinion/22220400_1_afghan-police-afghan-leader-hamid-karzai.

Patrick Cockburn, "The Warlords Casting a Shadow over Afghanistan," *Independent,* May 11, 2009. www.independent.co.uk/news/world/asia/the-warlords-casting-a-shadow-over-afghanistan-1682660.html.

James Dobbins, "Our Man in Kabul," *Foreign Affairs,* November 4, 2009. www.foreignaffairs.com/articles/65669/james-dobbins/our-man-in-kabul.

Fred Kaplan, "Has Karzai Gone Crazy?" *Slate,* April 5, 2010. www.slate.com/id/2249536.

Christian Le Mière, "Kabul's New Patron? The Growing Afghan-Chinese Relationship," *Foreign Affairs,* April 13, 2010. www.foreignaffairs.com/articles/66194/christian-le-miere/kabuls-new-patron.

Peter Oborne, "Back to the Dark Ages: How Life in Kabul Is Still Punctuated with Shootings, Assassinations, Kidnappings, and Bombings," *Daily Mail Online,* April 29, 2009. www.dailymail.co.uk/debate/article-1174647/PETER-OBORNE-Back-dark-ages-How-life-Kabul-punctuated-shootings-assassinations-kidnappings-bombings.html.

Alissa J. Rubin, "Karzai's Isolation Worries Afghans and the West," *New York Times,* June 7, 2010. www.nytimes.com/2010/06/08/world/asia/08afghan.html?ref=hamid_karzai.

Elizabeth Rubin, "Crazy Like a Fox," *Foreign Policy,* June 8, 2010. www.foreignpolicy.com/articles/2010/06/08/crazy_like_a_fox.

Chris Sands, "Afghanistan's Pashtuns Fight for Their Way of Life," *National,* July 11, 2010. www.thenational.ae/apps/pbcs.dll/article?AID=/20100712/FOREIGN/707119872/1002.

Nick Schifrin, "Afghan President Karzai Rallies His Troops," ABC News, June 13, 2010. http://abcnews.go.com/WN/Media/afghan-president-hamid-karzai-rallies-troops/story?id=10904699.

U.S. Department of State, "Background Note: Afghanistan," Bureau of South and Central Asian Affairs, March 26, 2010. www.state.gov/r/pa/ei/bgn/5380.htm.

Websites

Embassy of Afghanistan, Washington, D.C. (www.embassyofafghanistan.org). Informative resources include classroom lessons on Afghan history, arts, and culture; profiles of Hamid Karzai and his cabinet ministers; and an updated bibliography of books about Afghanistan past and present. Less balanced FAQs present an optimistic view of Afghan politics, economic reconstruction, national security, and tourism.

Good Afghan News (www.goodafghannews.com). Concerned that bad news about Afghanistan dominates the headlines, Afghan emigrant Abdullah Qazi created this site in 2009 to raise awareness of good things and real progress, however limited, happening in Afghanistan. Up-to-date reports on sports, job creation, education, environmental issues, women's rights, security, and reconstruction give an alternative perspective of a country at war.

Office of the President, Islamic Republic of Afghanistan (www.president.gov.af/index_eng.aspx). This official Afghan government site offers links to nearly sixty of Karzai's speeches, in English; transcripts of Karzai press conferences; and a wide array of official documents, including the Afghan constitution.

About the Author

Viqi Wagner is a textbook and legislative editor and a writer with a special interest in international politics. She lives and works in Richmond, Virginia.